GOLDEN CRADLE

Golden Cradle

How the Adoption Establishment Works— And How to Make It Work for You

Arty Elgart

with

Claire Berman

A Citadel Press Book
Published by Carol Publishing Group

Copyright © 1991 by Arty Elgart
All rights reserved. No part of this book may be reproduced in any form, except by a newspaper or magazine reviewer who wishes to quote brief passages in connection with a review.

A Citadel Press Book
Published by Carol Publishing Group
Citadel Press is a registered trademark of Carol Communications, Inc.

Editorial Offices: 600 Madison Avenue, New York, N.Y. 10022
Sales & Distribution Offices: 120 Enterprise Avenue, Secaucus, N.J. 07094
In Canada: Musson Book Company, a Division of General Publishing Company, Ltd., Don Mills, Ontario M3B 2T6

Queries regarding rights and permissions should be addressed to Carol Publishing Group, 600 Madison Avenue, New York, N.Y. 10022

Carol Publishing Group books are available at special discounts for bulk purchases, for sales promotions, fund raising, or educational purposes. Special editions can be created to specifications. For details contact: Special Sales Department, Carol Publishing Group, 120 Enterprise Avenue, Secaucus, N.J. 07094

Manufactured in the United States of America

10 9 8 7 6 5 4 3 2 1

Library of Congress Cataloging-in-Publication Data

Elgart, Arty
    Golden Cradle : how the adoption establishment works, and how to make it work for you / by Arty Elgart, with Claire Berman.
      p. cm.
    "A Citadel Press book."
    Includes bibliographical references.
    ISBN 0-8065-1261-X
    1. Adoption—United States. 2. Adoption agencies—United States.
I. Berman, Claire, II. Title.
HV875.55.E54 1991
362.7'33'0973—dc20
                                          91-16645
                                                CIP

To my son Josh
Born: Saturday, October 13, 1979
at the Edna Gladney Home, Fort Worth, Texas
I thank God every night for you.

****

And to Josh's birth parents . . . for making such a courageous and loving plan for Josh. It was your decision that inspired me to create Golden Cradle, which has changed the lives of thousands of people. I thank you with all my heart. May God bless you and watch over you.

Contents

Acknowledgments ix
Introduction xiii

PART I: **From Empty Nest to Golden Cradle: A Personal Reminiscence** 1

1. Why Me? 3
2. Spreading the Joy 15
3. Golden Cradle: From Maverick to Model Adoption Program 25

PART II: **A Candid Look at Adoption and Its Cast of Characters** 43

4. Why You? Confronting Infertility 45
5. Is Adoption the Answer? Facing Your Feelings and Confronting the Myths 56
6. The Truth About Birth Mothers 67
7. What Adoptive Applicants Look Like and What They Want to Know 89
8. Consider the Children 107
9. Addressing the Openness Issue 121

PART III: **Let's Do It!** 133

10. Working With an Agency 135
11. Pursuing an Independent Adoption 154
12. Adopting a Child From Another Land 176

13. How Do You Keep From Going Nuts While You Wait?   187

              Afterword   193
Appendix I: National Adoption Resources   191
Appendix II: Suggested Reading   203

Acknowledgments

CLAIRE BERMAN . . . For all your hard work and for taking the time to get to know me.

Blanche Schlessinger . . . For believing in me.

Carole Stuart . . . My editor.

The memory of my mother, Henrietta Elgart, who helped me become the person I am.

My father, Robert Elgart, who told me it was "The Stork" who brought babies.

Joan Olenick . . . My sister and friend. (Sorry I kicked you under the table all of those years.)

Louise Elgart . . . For thirteen years and two wonderful children.

MaryAnne Giello . . . Your warmth and support to me and to birth parents has helped Golden Cradle become what it is.

Nancy Gose . . . For the early years.

Marlene Piasecki and the Golden Cradle staff . . . For your dedication and willingness to always go the extra mile.

Gerri Carson and Helene Gummerman . . . For believing in me.

Golden Cradle Board Members . . . For your support, time, and dedication.

Birth Mothers and Birth Fathers . . . For small miracles.

Proud Parents . . . For giving and believing, not just receiving.

Larry Seidman, M.D. . . . For your care and passion for birth parents.

Tina (Twinkie's mom) . . . For your thoughtful comments and great ideas.

Steve Brody, Stuart Parmet, Elliot Stone, and Jo Cooper . . . For teaching me what friendship is all about.

Hesh Milakofsky and Tim Chromchak . . . Who helped carry the ball.

Suzanne St. Pierre . . . Who helped let the world know what we were doing.

Also, everyone I have not mentioned, but who has made a difference. You know who you are. My thanks and love to all of you.

Finally, my children, Josh and Abby. The two most wonderful kids any parent could ever have. You each entered my life in a different way; you have enhanced it in ways that you'll never know. I love you sooooooo much.

—ARTY ELGART

A book is written with the help and encouragement of many people. This one is no exception. First came Blanche Schlessinger, who asked me to help tell Arty's story. Julian Bach, my agent, sent the proposal on its way. And Carole Stuart, friend and editor, supported the work from start to finish.

The book could not have been written, however, without the cooperation and assistance of Marlene Piasecki, executive director of Golden Cradle, and the agency's staff members. At various times I turned to each of them for their knowledge and insights. At *all* times, they were generous and helpful. I feel fortunate to have been, for a time, part of the Golden Cradle family.

Golden Cradle's clients—birth parents and adoptive parents—were no less forthcoming, even when the interviews required them to share some very personal feelings and experiences. Many of their stories and comments appear in this book. I hope we have used them well.

My thanks to attorney Steve Sacharow for providing information and clarification as needed.

Mary Zagorski, Arty's secretary, was a friend at the other end of the line.

At home, I had the support of my husband, Noel Berman, and (somewhat far-flung at times) of my sons, Eric, Mitchell, and Orin Berman. I am *always* grateful for their caring.

Finally, a word about Arty Elgart. I first heard about Arty years ago when I worked for a national adoption center. Rumor had it that there was this maverick in Philadelphia—a man who had the audacity not only to arrange adoptions on his own but to *advertise*. The adoption establishment was aghast.
Over the years, I saw people's attitudes begin to change. They wanted to learn more about Arty Elgart and about Golden Cradle, the agency he created. Later, many also sought to learn *from* him. Indeed, several established agencies and private adoption facilitators are now engaged in some of the very same practices for which Arty had been criticized earlier—taking adoption public.
I have learned from Arty, too. In the process of collaboration, Arty and I have become not just coauthors but friends. It has been my privilege to help tell the story of Golden Cradle. I thank Arty and the agency for trusting me to do it right.

—CLAIRE BERMAN

Introduction

For years people had been telling me, "You ought to write a book about adoption."

"You're right," I would say, "I probably should." But I held off. For one thing, I was far too busy *living* adoption: enjoying the miracle of fatherhood that I had once feared might elude me forever. That's the family side of things. On the professional front, both my time and energy were directed toward building a major business out of a modest automotive accessories company that I had started together with my father. I was a brash kid from the streets of Frankford, a lower-middle-class neighborhood of row houses and warehouses in Philadelphia, who was making it by dint of hard work and a "can-do" attitude that has always stood me in good stead.

Once I became involved in adoption as a personal issue, that same can-do attitude led me to undertake a personal crusade: to change the face of adoption. I wanted to help others who were frustrated by an adoption establishment that often seemed more intent on keeping couples *from* adopting than on enabling them to form successful families. The effort to find and place babies needing families with couples eager to adopt them became incredibly time-consuming. And the subsequent challenge to convert a personal mission into an accredited adoption agency, Golden Cradle, took whatever ability and energy I had left. Looking back, I realize that it even took time that should have been given to my wife and children. I had become *that* obsessed.

So, yes, there was a need for a good, honest book about adoption. But, no, I couldn't add that task to a plate of projects that was already spilling over at the sides. "*Someday,*" I told myself and others, "*someday I will get around to it.*"

Then something happened that led me to take the "book" folder out of my files and mark it "current." That something has been widely publicized and described in the media—newspapers, magazines, television talk shows—as "the crisis in adoption." Briefly summarized, the crisis is this: Because of a number of factors, a situation has developed in which there are far more people trying to adopt healthy, white babies than the number of such babies being made available for adoption.

I became concerned about the panic and sense of hopelessness being felt by so many couples who wanted to create a family and who saw adoption as their only means to that end. I felt there was a need for a realistic book that would also be inspirational. Because, you see, I honestly believe that you can adopt if you really want to—that, one way or another (and we'll talk about those ways), your dreams of building a family through adoption *can* come true.

I also understand how even a *rumor* of a crisis in adoption can lead many husbands and wives to become desperate—willing to do anything, follow any path (however tortuous) to get a baby. And I want to say to those of you who are feeling that desperation, *Stop!* Don't panic. Don't say yes to anything that doesn't *feel* right to you. Don't go into international adoption if you don't want to. Don't attempt to adopt a baby because other people expect it, even if you'd feel more comfortable with an older child. Don't agree to an open adoption if you're not prepared to follow through.

Further, don't do anything that will make it difficult for you to look in the mirror the next morning . . . or to face your son or daughter several years down the line and tell that child how he or she came into your life. If something feels wrong *to* you, it is wrong *for* you. Adoption is not a one-time event. It is a *relationship.* But—and here's a big but—don't reject any of the possibilities that come your way until *after* you've looked into them, considered them, and know *why* this or that avenue isn't the right one for you.

I am also concerned about the birth mothers and the different pressures that the adoption crisis has brought to bear on them—either to place babies whom they wish to raise or (and this happens far more often than is acknowledged by the media) to keep babies when their youth and/or circumstances would favor a different decision. Adoption is not successful unless it is the right decision for *all* the parties involved.

Let's take a look for a moment at the crisis in adoption, at the factors that have contributed to its occurring now. Chief among them has been a tremendous increase, over the past twenty years, in the number of couples seeking help for infertility. It's not so much that the incidence of infertility has increased, explains William Mosher, Ph.D., a statistician with the National Center for Health Statistics, who has directed many of the studies. It's that a very large group of people who were born during the baby boom, the years between 1946 and 1964, are now twenty-six to forty-four years old—an age range where they are ready to be involved in childbearing. Thus, the number of couples who are concerned about childbirth has skyrocketed.

In large part, too, this same group of men and women have been marrying later than in the past and have been postponing parenthood until both partners feel secure that their careers are off the ground. Having children can wait, they believe. When they *are* ready, many discover that they may have waited too long. Added to delayed attempts to conceive, a silent epidemic of sexually transmitted diseases, prolonged use of the pill or IUD, and sterilization operations that cannot be reversed have hindered many people's ability to produce babies.

At the same time that more men and women are interested in adopting, greater numbers of young women who find themselves faced with pregnancies that they neither wished nor planned are choosing to keep and raise their babies rather than place them for adoption. I believe that, in large part, this is a result of a change in society's attitude toward women who have unplanned pregnancies and toward the babies they bear. In today's climate, young unwed mothers are better able to keep and raise their babies—and 94 percent of those who elect to carry their babies to term are making that choice.

Whether or not all of this will ultimately be for the better is something I do not know. But every time I read about some child being abused or murdered by a parent who is at the end of her rope, every time I turn on the TV and see a picture of some newborn baby turning up in a trash can (and then wonder about the discarded infants who have not been discovered), I cannot help but wish fervently that adoption had been presented to the mothers as a positive option for the babies they bore but were unable to nurture. I'm concerned that adoption has gotten a bum rap in some circles. I'd like this book to reach birth mothers and the people they turn to for help when faced with an unplanned pregnancy—parents, guidance counselors, doctors, nurses, clergy. I'd like them to understand adoption as an option. Moreover, I'd like them to know that (increasingly) making an adoption decision does not have to mean the end of all knowledge of the child, and can even lead to a continuing relationship with the adoptive family.

I'd like this book to reach people with infertility problems. I know, from personal experience, about the tensions that arise between husband and wife when "conceiving a baby" becomes a preoccupation instead of a pleasure. I know how insensitive one's doctors, family, and friends can be at a time when you need all the support and sensitivity, and then some, that it's possible for others to provide. I also know (as you will see from my personal story) that "infertility" is not necessarily a permanent condition. Although I'm an advocate of adoption, I don't think it's something for couples to rush into. There is a time to go for fertility testing and treatment. There is also a time, for many couples, to call it quits and go on with their lives.

I'd like to help men and women look at adoption realistically and decide whether it seems right for them. The next step, after finding out that you're unlikely to conceive a child, is not necessarily making application to adopt. Just as infertility happens to a couple, not just to either the husband or wife, so, too, does adoption happen to a couple. Do each of you, independently, want to have a child, or is one of you simply going along with the idea of adoption in order to appease the other? There's nothing wrong with a decision to remain child-free. What *is* wrong is going ahead with an adoption for all the wrong reasons. Keep in mind: It's not just the future of the marriage that's likely to be at stake in these cases; it's also the future of a child.

I'd like to use this book to do away with the mystique surrounding adoption, to shed light on some of the great unknowns. Once you are able to answer "yes" to the possibility of adopting, chances are you will want to know more: about the people who become adoptive parents; about the birth parents and their families; about the babies. After years of meeting and dealing with all of the parties, I'd like to introduce you to the real actors in the adoption drama—some of the finest people I've been privileged to meet.

I'd like my book to help couples go about the business of adopting, to offer information about the different ways of proceeding (through an agency, independently, across national borders), and to present the upsides and the downsides—as I see them—to each method.

When you first enter the adoption maze, you're likely to feel yourself blocked at every turn. As an adoptive parent, I have been where you are. You may move ahead blindly, going through any opening that seems to show promise. I can understand that, even though some of those openings lead into blind alleys from which you'll find yourself backtracking. Or they just don't take you to the place you want to be.

I have two feelings about adoption which may sound contradictory. The first is to leave no stone unturned, to check out every lead along an uncertain path. The second is to warn you against following a direction, however right it seems, when your instincts tell you there's a better way to go. If you find a door ajar, open it—see what's inside—but you don't necessarily have to enter the room. When it comes to adopting, my advice (and, believe me, it works) is: *Don't take no for an answer.* It is also: You don't have to say yes to the first guy who asks you to dance.

I'd like to use this book to help agencies move forward, too. I know that some readers out there in the "adoption establishment" will think it is presumptuous of me to offer advice. No matter that I've been an adoptive parent for more that twelve years and that the agency I founded, Golden Cradle, has recently celebrated its tenth anniversary . . . no matter that many of the innovations we created are now routinely used by other agencies (even those that initially criticized them) . . . when it comes to adoption, in certain circles I am still regarded as the new kid on the block.

As a parent, however, I have been taught something: there's a great deal that you can learn from kids. They often have a refreshing ability to wade through a lot of trash and come up with the truth. And the truth here is that, while a lot of agencies have taken tremendous steps toward improving their procedures, toward fostering greater openness among the parties to an adoption, toward the inclusion of birth parents *and* adoptive applicants in the decision-making process, there are still too many agencies that remain tradition-bound, that make those who wish to adopt feel like supplicants instead of applicants, and that fail to create a general atmosphere in which adoption can flourish—before, during, and after placement.

So there you have it, my reasons for writing this book now.

If you are reading it because you are considering adoption as a way of building a family, I'd feel privileged if you'd let me join you as your friend and guide.

If you are expecting a baby and wondering about making an adoption plan, I am confident that you will find in these pages some sense of the possibilities.

If your connection to adoption is professional, I hope we can work together toward improving a service that is ever challenging, life-enhancing, and deserving of the very best efforts we have to give.

If you are a general reader, I hope that gaining a greater understanding of adoption will leave you enriched—as my son Josh and my daughter Abby (who came to me through different doors) enrich my life, every day, every hour, every minute.

Before we go forward together on the journey to adoption, however, it may help to understand just where I am coming from. I invite you first to join me in looking back.

I

From Empty Nest to Golden Cradle: A Personal Reminiscence

1

Why Me?

Most kids don't grow up thinking, *Someday when I'm older, I'm going to marry and become an adoptive parent.* I was no exception. As a boy, if I thought about the future at all, it was in terms of having to work. That's what grown men did, it seemed to me, and everything else in life was incidental. That's the way I ran my own life for a long time, too.

My father, Robert, set the example. From the time he was in the eighth grade, and his father, my grandfather, made him quit school so he could help out in the family delicatessen, my dad had done nothing *but* work. So closely connected was his livelihood to the life of our family—my mother, Henrietta, kid sister, Joan, and me—that, for much of my childhood, we even lived over the family store: a retail auto-supply business located on a street of similar shops and warehouses. Although my Mom had a master's degree in physical education and taught school, my idea of parents' roles was that Dad worked to put food on the table, and Mom prepared the food.

When I entered my teens, our family moved to Mt. Airy, a northwestern suburb of Philadelphia. Dad had sold the store and become involved in a new venture: every Friday, Saturday, and Sunday he sold auto supplies at a farmers' market in New Castle, Delaware. Frequently, the weekends would find me working beside him.

Dad was not a loving father, although I think he did love me and just didn't know how to show it in an affectionate manner.

He didn't know how to hug. Instead, he would give me things, and then he would take them away whenever we disagreed. And we often disagreed. I think it was a relief to both of us when, at the age of sixteen and a half, I went away to Valley Forge Military Academy. At the local high school, I'd spent more time in the marching band (where I played the trumpet, the euphonium, and the baritone horn) and playing on the basketball and soccer teams than I'd spent on my studies. Valley Forge provided the structure that helped me better organize my time.

After six months, active duty in the Army reserves following my high school graduation, off I went to Missouri State University in Kirksville, Missouri. Although I had managed to put some geographic distance between my father and me, his work ethic had lodged in my soul, along with a need for me to show that I could be independent of him. I worked three jobs a semester—in a pizza store, furniture warehouse, and a snack shop (where I put in two hours a day in exchange for two meals)—while earning a degree that would enable me to become a physical education teacher, like my mom. But even after I came home and began to teach, I was drawn back to the family business, working every weekend at the farmers' market. Eventually, I left teaching to work at the business full time. I never took the time to go out and smell the roses. I never planned a future. The way I looked at things then was: You work and life *happens* (although sometimes not as quickly as you'd like it to).

I was almost thirty-two in September 1973 when I married Louise (Weezie), twenty-six, whom I met on a blind date. Weezie was (still is) an English teacher. She was, and still is, a very neat lady. Unfortunately, in April 1987, after thirteen and a half years of marriage, we decided to part, but to this day we remain good friends and cooperating parents.

It's the parent part that I want to recall for you now. Like most newlywed couples, Weezie and I didn't really think about kids. We just assumed it was going to happen once we were ready. And, again like most couples, we weren't ready right away. In fact, Weezie was taking birth control pills—which I've since learned is common with people who later run into fertility problems. You're tinkering with the body; it can screw up your system.

Because I'd married late, we didn't wait all that long before we began "trying," which in our case simply meant doing away with any precautions. At first, you take for granted that this means you're going to get pregnant soon and then you'll decide when you're going to have the next one. One month goes by . . . two months, six months . . . nine months go by and nothing's happening. You start looking at each other. *How come nothing's happening?*

Other people are even less tactful. They say things like, "You two guys going to have a child soon?" and you find yourself saying something like, "Yeah, well, I'm taking this correspondence course in how-to." Then you chuckle and that's the end of *that* conversation. It's almost like being in a room with a bee. The bee's buzzing around and you don't want to get stung, so you just walk out of the room. You just want to chuck it and dismiss it. Psychologists would say you're using denial.

Going the Infertility-Testing Route

A year goes by, and denial no longer works, so you make an appointment with a doctor. You also start thinking, *Why me?* Why am I sitting here in this doctor's office talking about the kinds of things that should be nobody's business but mine and Weezie's? "*Why me?*" is the beginning of the acknowledgment that there just may be a problem. It is the critical question that starts you on a search for solutions. "*Why me?*" begins the story of my own life in adoption.

"*Why us?*" is the question that Weezie and I asked of one another when we ran up against problems of infertility and started going to Dr. Abe Rakoff for tests. Talk about fun! Talk about how it feels to have a doctor look at your scrotum to see if you have a varicocele (an enlarged or dilated vein in the spermatic cord within the scrotum, like a varicose vein in the leg), the most common, identifiable cause of male infertility. Yes, I had a varicocele, but it might not be the cause of our problems. One couldn't be sure.

Talk about taking a sperm test. You're thirty-three years old, and you're asking the doctor, "How do you do a sperm test?"

"Best time to do it is in the morning, use a small cup, and you have to be over here for the test within thirty to forty-five minutes," he says. So you figure out how to do a sperm test. Then, with your package concealed in a paper bag that's as anonymous looking as you can manage, you get in the car and speed off, hoping that you don't get stopped by a traffic cop along the way and have to explain to him what the emergency is.

The encounter you have with the nurse in the doctor's office is tough enough. Trying to be as inconspicuous as possible, you silently hand over your package. "What *is* this?" she asks, her voice at a volume that could easily make it to the second balcony of just about any theater in the land.

Still trying to be discreet, and struggling to avoid the gaze of the patient who walked in after you and now stands waiting behind you, you whisper, "It's a sperm test."

"What's that? I didn't hear it," says the nurse, her voice even louder, if possible.

You're thinking, *You should have heard me the first time, you bitch*, but you say again, "It's a sperm test. It has to be taken care of right away," wishing there was a hole you could crawl into. And that's only one of the dehumanizing things that happen to people in pursuit of procreation.

The other stressful thing is what "trying to have a baby" does to the relationship between a couple. For one thing, lovemaking takes a different turn. It's no longer "lovemaking." Instead, it's "sex." And it's not a part of "romancing" any more. Instead, it's what you do "to have a baby." These are the kinds of things that settle in. And if you're a noncommunicative couple, you don't talk about these things, these feelings. Infertility does a number on couples in a very quiet way. It causes problems.

But something happened during the fertility-testing process that led me to take my first steps toward adoption. They weren't very successful steps, however.

Dr. Rakoff's wife, a nice lady, would show up at his office about once or twice a week to counsel couples about adoption if they were having infertility problems. One day, she brought out a bunch of three-by-five cards and handed them to me. They contained the names and addresses of agencies dealing in adoption: Lutheran Services, Catholic Family Services, an agency handling adoptions in South America. I remember asking her, "Do you have pamphlets from any of these places?" She reached into the drawer of her desk, and handed me a brochure to look at. It was from the Edna Gladney Home in Ft. Worth, Texas.

I'm a people person, so the first thing I did was turn to the back of the brochure where the board of directors was listed, zeroing in on the name of a woman who had a Villanova, Pennsylvania address. I memorized her name and, as soon as I left the office, looked up her phone number and placed a call to her home. It turned out that she and her husband had adopted three children from Gladney, and that she headed the Edna Gladney Auxiliary in the area.

Weezie and I visited her at her home. We met her husband. He had on a military uniform. I talked to him about my military school background. I thought we had hit it off, and confidently sent off a letter to Gladney expressing our interest in adopting. A month later, their response came back. Our application had been turned down.

On the Adoption Trail

After almost a year of seeing Dr. Rakoff, I decided to nose my way into adoption beyond this one application, which had been sent out almost as a feeler while we were still hopeful that the fertility treatments would succeed. As time passed, it was very clear to us that conceiving a child was much less important than the opportunity to link our lives with a child, and love a child. We wanted to be a family very much—and so we began seriously to explore adoption.

I started my search at Philadelphia's main library, where I found only three books on adoption. One was copyrighted

1947, one 1955, and one didn't seem very useful. I also didn't know anyone I could turn to for advice, because—this was 1975—people didn't talk a lot about adoption, and I didn't think I knew anyone who had adopted children. (Later, I found out that several children who I thought had been born into their families had in fact joined their families through adoption.) Nobody was there to give me information or to hold my hand through this emotional journey I was now entering upon, as I hope to be able to do for you in this book.

Next, I got hold of a phone book and started calling attorneys, doctors, gynecologists. I phoned over a hundred different agencies . . . in California, Arizona, Vermont . . . You name the state, I called the agencies. Canada, Mexico . . . There wasn't even a category for "Adoption" in the classified directory (later, I was the one to change that situation in my area), so I looked under Social Service Agencies, and phoned those that seemed as if they might be appropriate. I filled five pages of a legal pad.

"Why *not* me?" is the question I then found myself asking, as I telephoned agency after agency only to be discouraged at every turn. For the most part when I called the agencies, I was treated like dirt. I felt as if I was interrupting the people I reached at the other end from reading the newspaper. And yet these were social workers, people who went to school to learn to help other human beings. Mind you, this is not an indictment against social workers, but I have to tell this as I experienced it. Even now, you may be experiencing much the same thing.

Here is a typical phone conservation: "Hi," I'd say. "My name is Arthur Elgart. Can I speak to someone, please, concerning adoption?"

"Well, we don't do that many adoptions, but . . . let me see who does. . . . Well, I think Mrs. Brown handles that. Hold on please." And so you hold . . . and hold. Finally, she comes back on the line. "Mr. Elgart, I'm sorry, but Mrs. Brown doesn't handle adoption. Mrs. Jones does, but she's not here right now."

I'd say, "I can respect that, but will she be back soon? Is she on vacation? Is there anyone else who can help?"

"Well, I think she's . . . wait a second . . . let me double-check. . . ."

I'm on hold . . . on hold . . . on hold. It seemed like my life was on hold. We were on hold with infertility, we were on hold with the baby, we were on hold with sex because we had to do it at a certain time, and now I call an agency to adopt . . . and I'm on hold again.

"Mrs. Jones is on vacation. She'll be back next week. Do you want to call her back?"

I'd say, "Would you mind taking my number? Maybe she'll call *me* back." (I quickly learned that you don't leave your name at agencies. They *don't* call you back.)

At another agency, I would be asked, "Do you know how many calls we get, Mr. Elgart?"

"No, I don't know how many calls you get."

"Well, we get hundreds and hundreds of calls to adopt, and there just aren't children around."

"Listen," I'd say, "what happens to all these women who are getting pregnant? I taught school. We had high school juniors and seniors, even sophomores, who were pregnant. What happens to those kids and to their babies?"

"Well, they either keep their kids or have an abortion."

"I can understand that," I'd say, "but there has to be a third element. What about people who go too long for an abortion and cannot keep the babies? And what about those who make a conscious decision to see the pregnancies through but cannot raise their babies?" It was like talking to the wind.

I contacted every social service agency in the five-county Philadelphia area. The Catholic agency wouldn't see us because we weren't of their faith. The Jewish agency wouldn't see us because, they told us, they had "very few, extremely few" babies and "very long, extremely long" lists of couples waiting to adopt.

I was concerned about *my* biological timetable now. I was approaching thirty-four, and making four, five, six calls a day, without success. Why *not* us? Why couldn't two such nice people as Weezie and I be entrusted with a child whom we would promise to nurture and love for the rest of our lives? Gradually, I was growing to hate the system. I hated the agencies' remarks: "There's very little hope" . . . "We only serve couples of our faith" . . . "We don't do many adoptions" . . . "You're thirty-two or thirty-three or thirty-four. There's a five-year waiting list. You'll be too old by the time you get to the top of the list." I felt so frustrated. There I was, a former phys-ed instructor who had spent so much time being around other people's children, facing the possibility of living my life without kids.

I said, "Bullshit." And I persevered. I didn't even tell Weezie how many calls I placed because we'd already been through so much during our fertility examinations. I just said that I was looking into adoption and, "no luck yet."

Like the Ancient Mariner, I felt called upon to tell my story to everyone—from my barber to the guys I played ball with. I took on two of society's secrets and made them public. First: "Weezie and I are unable to have a child" (baring our infertility) and, second, "We're looking to adopt." Secrecy had long been viewed as the cornerstone of adoption. But I've learned that couples have to be very forthcoming about the fact that they are trying to adopt. That, after all, is the way we realized our dream of becoming parents. Eventually.

Some Side Excursions

As part of the process of searching for a baby to adopt, I also contacted several lawyers whose names were given to me by friends and acquaintances. I thought they might have contacts with pregnant women and could serve as intermediaries between the women who planned to place their babies for adoption and couples who planned to adopt. Nothing happened.

Along the way, I realized that if you put a little grease on the axle, the train can run nice and smooth. People don't like to talk about black-market adoption—the payment of money for a baby over and above the costs of medical and legal services—but we all know that it exists. I couldn't do it.

When the opportunity came my way, I'll admit it was tempting. First there was a call from a lawyer in Detroit. He'd heard I was looking for a baby, and could help me out. It would cost ten thousand dollars, in cash—and, no, he had no information about the baby. I passed.

Next came a phone call from an attorney in Bucks County, Pennsylvania. He'd been given my number by one of the lawyers I'd phoned originally. A baby was available for adoption, he told me. Was I interested? It would cost twenty-five thousand dollars.

"Can you tell me anything about the child?" I asked.

"It's a boy. He was just born," he answered.

"Can you tell me anything about the medical history?"

"No," he said. "We don't have information like that."

"Is the baby healthy?"

"Yes."

I said, "Why is it so expensive—do hospital bills run that high?" At that time, the obstetrical fee for a normal delivery was about four hundred dollars and hospitals were charging about fourteen hundred dollars for a three-day stay, so you're looking at about two thousand dollars on the high side. It was obvious where the rest of the money was going.

Weezie and I could have managed to come up with the money. We *would* have managed it if the money had gone to cover legitimate legal fees and medical expenses. But this wasn't right. The money I was being asked to hand over to the attorney didn't have anything to do with counseling. There was no support there for either the birth mother or for the adoptive couple. In five, ten, twenty years down the line, if the attorney died and we or the child needed information about the biological parents and their medical history, there'd be no way of getting it. That information would have gone to its grave along with the intermediary. There was no continuity.

All that this was about was the transfer of a child. Even then, however, I knew that there was much more to adoption than getting a baby. I was also concerned that, somewhere during our lives together, my son would look at me and ask, "Dad, what did you pay for me?" And I would have to tell him. I used the same sense that has helped me all my years in business—the sense that, if it doesn't feel right, pass. Once again, I passed.

Still, it hurt to say no. For a while I had trouble sleeping. But Weezie and I continued with our quest to adopt. We were convinced that somewhere there had to be a child for us—just as you, must be convinced that, despite disappointments along the way, there *will* be a child for you.

The event that turned *our* lives around was a party I attended in Albany, New York, on November 14, 1977. It was given by my sister Joan and her husband, Stan, to celebrate the second birthday of their son, Brett. Weezie was unable to make it, so I went alone. Except for the birthday boy and his father, I was the only man at the party. The other guests were mostly mothers and their little kids.

I found myself seated next to an attractive woman named Donna whose husband was a medical school classmate of my brother-in-law. She asked if my children were at the party. I said, "I don't have any children, but my wife and I are hoping to adopt." Listening to Donna speak, I knew for certain that she hadn't grown up in, or anywhere near, Albany. More to make conversation than anything else, I asked where she was from.

"Dallas, Texas," she replied.

"That's a coincidence," I told her. "My wife and I applied to an adoption agency in Ft. Worth, the Edna Gladney Home, but they wouldn't work with us."

I believe in *bashert* (the Yiddish word for fate or "meant to be"). Here I was, a fellow from Philadelphia, Pennsylvania, who had traveled to attend a two-year-old's birthday party in Albany, New York, and found himself seated next to a woman from Dallas, Texas, who turned to me and said, "The fellow I used to go with before my marriage is an attorney in Ft. Worth. I think he's affiliated with the Gladney Home."

She wrote his number down for me. When I phoned him, the lawyer said that he was sorry . . . I'd been misinformed about his having a connection to the Gladney Home . . . but he *did* have a friend who worked for the law firm that represented Gladney. "Would you do me a favor?" I asked this man whom I had never met. "Would you speak to your friend about our hopes to adopt—and would you speak about me as if I were your oldest and best friend?" I then proceeded to give him a whole history of my wife and me.

The Process

A week later, we received an application form from the Gladney Home, which we filled out and returned the next morning, special delivery. In late January, there was a phone call from Gladney, informing us that their representative would be in our area to interview us and two other couples. In May, all three couples gathered at St. Davids Inn in St. Davids, Pennsylvania, where the representative explained to us what Gladney was about. The meeting lasted an hour and a half. We were told that the cost of adoption would be about $3800 plus $976 round-trip airfare for two (to pick up the baby). Interestingly, the Home did not use outside hospitals. The birth mothers delivered in a building on the campus.

In November 1978, we flew to Texas to attend a meeting of adoptive applicants. It was held at the Gladney Home, a handsome brick building situated on a beautiful campus in the middle of a rundown neighborhood. There were twenty-eight couples in all. We sat on bleachers in an auditorium. Several birth mothers spoke to us of their feelings about adoption. We asked questions, and received answers.

It was very comforting, because until then adoption had been a mystery to us, like going into a tunnel without a flashlight. Adoption? Well, you get somebody else's baby. That sounds okay, because all you want is a baby. You don't think about the sex of the child, about his or her medical history, about background. You don't give any thought to how (and whether) to someday tell your child that he or she is adopted. You don't know if you should ask a question. Maybe it will sound stupid, and they'll throw you out. Maybe your tie is crooked and that will cause "them" (the people who have the power to determine your fate) to look at you in a strange way. Who knows? We'd been under a microscope for the past several years. We didn't know what people were looking for when they looked at us or what they might now find that would lead them to declare us unfit.

At the meeting's close, we were told that we'd all have a baby within a year. We would have no choice in the sex. It was a little shocking. It's almost like someone stuck a needle in you and said, "Don't worry. You're gonna feel good soon." You can't believe it. That evening, Weezie and I flew back to Philadelphia. We didn't talk much.

On October 22, 1979, we received a phone call from LaVerne McGowen, the social worker assigned to us by Gladney. "Guess what," she told us. "You have a son."

We named him Joshua.

2

Spreading the Joy

From the moment we'd been accepted as a "Gladney family," Weezie and I had felt confident that our long wait would be over: there would soon be a child to fill the empty space in our home and in our hearts. And then a curious thing happened. Suddenly, it seemed as if all the calling cards I had been handing out over the years were producing results.

A few months after our home study had been completed, but before our son Josh was born, we received two phone calls about available babies in one week. Monday's call, from a gynecologist we knew, concerned a newborn boy who needed to be placed. Everything about the situation was comfortable and aboveboard. Had this opportunity come up earlier, there's no question that we would have taken it. But we passed on it this time because we were confident that Gladney would come through. Weezie and I liked the idea of working with an accredited agency. We also hoped that, having established a relationship with Gladney, we could go back to them for a second child when the time and circumstances were right.

The second phone call was from an osteopathic physician I'd been in touch with earlier in our search for a child. He, too, had a baby boy for us, and again we said no for the same reasons. In both cases, I had feelings of pleasure in knowing that the baby was going to go to another couple. Someone else would be made happy.

The next call came a few months later. It was from Gladney, and it was harder to deal with. A baby had just been born, they told us, whom we could adopt. They added that although the infant seemed fine, there were indications of a medical condition which might result in the child's developing a kidney problem as he grew older. Weezie and I discussed the situation and told the agency that we did not wish to take that chance.

It wasn't an easy decision for us to make. What if a baby was born to us, we asked ourselves, and *that* child was found to have a disabling condition at birth or later developed problems requiring special attention? There was no question, we knew, that we would love any child who entered our home, however he or she got there, and we'd do everything in our power to care for the child. But that was one of the upsides of adopting, we told ourselves. We did have a choice. Still, we were uneasy. Had we made the right decision in this case? Also, given our refusal, would Gladney still want to work with us? We continued to place our trust in the agency. We also continued to wait.

A few months went by before the next offer came our way. It was made by a nurse. She'd heard about our search, she said, and was trying to help out a young woman who was due to deliver soon and planned to place her baby for adoption. The nurse had promised the birth mother that she would find a good family for the baby. Again, medical and legal fees were the only costs to be assumed by the adopting parents. Were we interested?

Once again I explained our situation—that we were working with an agency in Texas and expected to become parents soon. Then I added that we knew of a couple in Pittsburgh who might be very interested in adopting the child. Would it be all right to have them contact her? She agreed.

I don't know what made me suggest another match *this* time, instead of just passing up the opportunity as I'd done in past, but the image of Mel and Hillary Feinberg, cousins of good friends of ours, just came into my head. I knew the Feinbergs had been married for a while, and I knew that they had been contacting agencies and lawyers about adopting, without success. I placed a call to Mel and Hillary, explained the situation, and gave them the nurse's phone number. Then I left for the airport. I was scheduled to attend an automotive accessories show in Chicago that week.

> Hillary Feinberg: We were thrilled when Arty called us. After seven years of marriage and trying to get pregnant, and then trying to adopt, we jumped at the possibility and wasted no time in getting in touch with the nurse. She asked us to write a resumé about ourselves, our work, our connections to the community, our feelings about family. She was wonderful. She personally knew the birth mother and was very concerned that the baby would be going to a good home. Within a week, the baby—our wonderful daughter Bari—was born. After picking her up from the hospital, we went home, set up a nursery, and phoned Arty with the news: we were a family.

On Sunday night I arrived home from Chicago bone-tired. It was 9:30 P.M., I remember, and I was already in bed when the phone rang. It was an ecstatic Mel and Hillary Feinberg, each on a different extension, their words tripping over one another as they told me with more joy than I had ever heard before: "It's a girl! She's here! And she's ours!" There were no words to express their gratitude, they said.

And how did *I* feel? As I listened to the Feinbergs, tears started coming out of my eyes. My heart was literally pounding against my rib cage. It was a feeling I never, ever had in my life. It was a tremendous feeling. Just at that time, Weezie came into the room. I put my hand over the receiver and I said, "It's Mel and Hillary from Pittsburgh. They just adopted a girl."

Realistically, that baby could have been ours, yet knowing that she was with the Feinbergs—knowing that I could make someone else happy—was such a nice feeling. Before that phone call, I never knew what it *sounded* like to make someone happy. Now I knew. I remember hanging up the phone and saying to Weezie, "This is so fantastic. I want to do it again!"

And I have done it again—about 953 times.

First Steps

Here's how my formal involvement in facilitating adoptions began. Weezie and I had recently adopted Josh, and I had this feeling: I wanted to do something for others in gratitude for our son—the wonderful gift that had been given to us. I belong to a group called Golden Slipper, a nonprofit organization comprised of successful businessmen and professionals who are pledged to give something back to the community. So one day, sitting in my office at the auto supply warehouse, I placed a call to a fellow Golden Slipper member, and suggested that the group inaugurate a program to help both adopting couples and birth mothers; we could help form families.

The project I proposed was based on the application of business principles to solve a social problem. I remembered what the agencies had told Weezie and me: there aren't any babies. And I knew what my gut told me: there had to be expectant mothers out there who, for one reason or another, could not take on the responsibilities of parenting. At the same time, they didn't know how to go about making a placement plan for their babies short of being interrogated by a social service agency and sent to wait out their pregnancies in the institutional setting of a home for unwed mothers. There had to be a better way. But first I had to reach the birth mothers.

What do you do in business? You advertise. My idea was that Golden Slipper would run ads directed to birth mothers who were considering adoptive placement. We would act as facilitators between them and couples wishing to adopt. Of course, we'd cover the cost of the ads and there would be no fee for our services. Adopting couples would be responsible only for doctor and hospital charges plus legal fees—payments that they would handle themselves.

If you haven't been personally involved in the indignities and inconsistencies of the adoption system, if you haven't had to navigate the detours and ignore the Stop signs, you couldn't understand the critical need for an adoption program that would cut through the protocol and get to the heart of the matter. The fellow on the other end of the line had not been in my shoes. Consequently, I wasn't surprised to hear him say that he didn't see adoption as an issue for Golden Slipper to take on.

Okay, I remember thinking as I replaced the receiver in its cradle, *I'll have to do it alone*. If I want something bad enough, I roll up my sleeves and go for it. I don't take no for an answer! My first step was to contact the office of the state attorney general in Harrisburg. I learned that as long as I didn't accept money or favors, private placement was legal. I also obtained a copy of the Pennsylvania adoption code, and memorized it word for word.

PREGNANT? *Phone (215) 289-BABY*

Next, I devised an ad that I would place in local papers, and had a special telephone installed in my office at the warehouse, which was then (in November 1979) being moved to the larger quarters that we occupy today. The telephone number was (215) 289-2229. (It was no coincidence that 2229 spells baby.) My first ad read: "PREGNANT? Young couple desires to adopt baby. Call Mary, 289-2229."

I ran the same ad in four different local newspapers, changing only the contact name in each: Mary, Susan, Marsha, Janet. That way, I'd find out which paper achieved the best response. The newspapers never had an ad like this before, but they didn't turn it down. I paid for all the ads myself. I was ready to do a boiler-room adoption service out of my office.

I believe that people make things happen. But I also believe there are certain coincidences in life—like meeting the woman from Texas at my nephew's birthday party—that set the stage for many important happenings. I can't explain it, but I certainly can acknowledge the mysterious workings of fate in my life—like the way I met my first adoptive couple.

All the while that I'd been speaking to the fellow from Golden Slipper, a factory representative named Jerry Gordon had been seated in my office, patiently waiting for me to get on with placing an order for automotive repair manuals. Partly to apologize for making him wait and partly to vent my frustration, I told him about my wanting to facilitate adoptions. I not only needed to reach birth mothers, but I needed to find couples who would trust me to act as an intermediary in their adoptions. It turned out that Jerry had a friend, Bonnie Strauss, who knew a couple, Karen and Michael Wagner, who were looking to adopt. He told Bonnie Strauss about me. She passed the information on. It wasn't long before I got a call from the Wagners.

> Karen Wagner: Michael and I had been married for nine years when we contacted Arty. It was certainly not our first effort to adopt. Along the way, we had explored Colombian adoption, but that did not work out. We also had been to a lawyer who arranged private adoptions. When the time came for us to make a deposit for his services, we pulled back. Something about the setup just didn't seem right. Then Bonnie Strauss told us about Arty—I think she described him as "this man who had some contacts and was interested in meeting couples who wanted to adopt"—and we phoned him. The way we saw it, this was as good a lead as any.

I heard from the Wagners on November 19, a Monday morning. I thought it would be a good idea for us to meet and asked when they could come in. "Right away," they answered. At three o'clock that same afternoon, a nice-looking coupled entered my office. I don't know which of us was the more nervous. I shook Michael's hand, gave Karen a kiss on the cheek, and asked them to sit down. What was going through my mind was: how do I judge, and who the hell *am* I to judge? But, dammit, if you're going to do something like this, you've got to be able to make some judgments. I honestly don't remember what I asked them. My basic criteria were that the couples I would work with be at least twenty-five years of age, have been married a minimum of three years, and have a bona fide infertility problem.

> Karen: Arty asked us how long we were married, about our infertility, and about our other attempts to adopt. He asked if we could financially afford to adopt and raise a child. By that time, Michael and I had filled out enough adoption applications to have ready answers to Arty's questions. We were

waiting for the hard ones, but they never came. I remember asking Arty, "Is *that* all the questions you have for us?"

"Give me a break," he answered, grinning. "I'm new at this."

Arty then told us that he did not have a child for us, but that he did have contact with a nurse who had promised to get in touch with him when she came across a situation (as periodically happened in her work) where a birth mother asked for help in placing a child. He also was involved in placing ads, and hoped to have birth mothers contact him directly.

The Wagners asked me what I charged. I said, "Nothing." I saw their heads go back, like they were thinking, *What are we getting into?* I proceeded to tell them that I wanted them to pay the medical bills directly to the hospital. I also told them they could use my attorney, who charged three hundred dollars for the legal work, or anybody else of their choosing. They asked if I wanted them to reimburse me for the ads I was taking out. "Sorry," I said. "I can't take any money. It's against the law." At the close of the interview, I remember telling the Wagners, "I *will* get back to you. I just don't know when."

> Karen: We had liked Arty right away. He was open and honest. Our senses of humor meshed. After leaving Arty's office, Michael and I went to a French restaurant we liked. We ordered a bottle of wine and toasted our future family. It was just before Thanksgiving and we were thankful. We just knew that Arty was going to get us a baby.

Five days into the new year, 1980, the nurse called to tell me that a baby girl had just been born to a twenty-nine-year-old mother. The woman was married and had three other children. The couple was going through a difficult time, and could not afford to care for this new child. The woman, who'd gone into labor while visiting her mother, knew no one else in town and asked the nurse for help in arranging an adoption with a good family. The nurse asked me if I knew of a couple who wished to adopt. "Oh, yes," I remember saying, "I have one couple in particular who would be suitable." At the time, one couple was *all* I had. I gave the nurse the Wagners' number.

After waiting what seemed like an eternity for the Wagners to receive the news, I phoned them, asking, "Did you get the call?" I really didn't have to ask. I heard the answer in their voices the minute they picked up the receiver. We were all so excited. We arranged to meet the following day to pick up the baby. I don't know how I managed to get any work done that day. I couldn't wait until it was time to go. As I left the office, my secretary, Mary, asked where I was going. I looked at her with a smile and said, "I'm going to make a delivery." I remembered my father telling me when I was a child that storks delivered babies. In a sense, that was what I was now going to do.

A Slight Case of Paranoia

What happened next serves as a good example of the hush-hush way in which adoption was handled not so very long ago. (I wish I could tell you that this kind of scene no longer takes place, but I'd be lying if I did.) The hospital was seven minutes from my office. When I drove up in my station wagon, Michael and Karen, along with Karen's mother, were already waiting in the parking lot.

The nurse, a lovely lady, came out to meet us. I went up to her and introduced myself. She said, "I've heard nice things about you, but I just have to ask you something again for my own conscience. You're not getting paid for this, are you?"

After I assured her that I would receive nothing from this but the personal satisfaction of helping to create a family, she met the Wagners and told them, "Wait by the back door of the hospital and we'll bring the baby to you."

I asked why.

"That's the way we handle adoptions," she said.

I asked her, "Isn't anybody going to show the Wagners how to clean the umbilical cord, put the diapers on, what to do with the powder?" These were simple common-sense questions that came into my mind.

Spreading the Joy

She said, "We don't do that here."

"What if this weren't an adoption? Would the parents of a newborn baby otherwise be shown how to do these things?"

She said, "Yes." Then she asked, "Did the couple bring a white or yellow blanket?" She didn't want the blanket's color to give away the sex of the baby.

"I don't think so," I answered. "I think they brought a pink one."

"Well, we'll try to conceal it as best we can," she said.

"Why all the secrecy?" I asked.

"In case the birth mother's family is in the parking lot copying the license plate number down," she answered. This was the way many people thought about adoption at that time.

Make no mistake about it, this same mentality continues to exist today, even though the media attention to greater openness in adoption might lead you to think otherwise. Just the other day, for example, a brochure prepared by an attorney who handles private adoptions came across my desk. Included in the advice this attorney gives to couples on how to achieve a successful adoption are "three steps to protect your privacy."

Step number one instructs adoption hopefuls to "Decide on a fictitious last name." Step two advises them to rent a post office box with an address instead of a number, so that anyone who corresponds with them will believe they are reaching a home address. The third step instructs couples to install an unlisted telephone number in their home, under the fictitious name chosen in step number one.

I find something terribly wrong with this cloak-and-dagger approach to adoption. Reason number one is that I believe that the birth parents deserve better. They deserve to be treated honestly and fairly. Reason number two is that I'm concerned that this kind of paranoia may continue well after the adoption arrangements have been made and placement has occurred. It's no fun to be constantly looking over your shoulder for a bogeyman who you feel might invade your home and snatch your baby. It makes you tense—and that tension is communicated to the child. My third reason for feeling uncomfortable with so much secrecy surrounding an adoption is that I think it conveys a subtle message: the reason for keeping anything secret is because you're ashamed of it.

On the contrary, when I looked at the Wagners on that day in January, 1980, the overriding emotions that I witnessed were happiness and pride. I never will forget the look on the face of Karen's mother, who had been handed the baby by the nurse, as she gazed down at her beautiful new granddaughter, and then gently placed the pink-wrapped bundle into the waiting arms of her daughter. With that gesture, it seemed to me, she was also passing on the honorable role of motherhood, with its obligations and privileges. It still gives me goose bumps to recall it.

But I don't have that scene only in my memory; I also own a photograph of it. Beginning a tradition that continues to this day, I had asked the Wagners to bring a camera with them when they picked up the baby. "The one thing that I want from you is the picture of the family," I said to them, as a spur-of-the-moment request. "I think *that's* my fee," I added, "so make it a big one."

That eight-by-ten photograph adorns the wall of my office. It has become the centerpiece of a collage containing close to a thousand similar photographs. For the word soon was out: I was doing adoptions.

I thought, "I'd better give this project a name." Golden Slipper came quickly to mind: an organization that gives something back to the community. And so I named my adoption project Golden Cradle. After all, I was giving something back for Josh.

3

Golden Cradle: From Maverick to Model Adoption Program

This book is written to encourage and assist you on the road to successful adoption. Yet, I'd be remiss as your guide on this tension-filled journey if I failed to tell you something about this entity named Golden Cradle—about how we did adoption differently from the start, about how our program evolved (and about how my thinking about adoption changed too, in certain respects, along the way). In a real sense, my history and the history of Golden Cradle are my credentials as your counselor.

It Pays to Advertise

I believe in advertising. If you want something, anything, let enough people know about it, and the chances are good that somebody will turn up to help you out. That's how the real world works. (It's only in fairy tales that the prince comes calling uninvited.) The first adoption I facilitated bore this out. Both the nurse and the Wagners had heard from different sources about the work I hoped to be doing. That was word-of-mouth advertising, and it brought results.

Next, I concentrated on creating and placing ads that would reach an audience of birth mothers. The small personal notices I began with were soon replaced by larger ads which I then placed in a wider range of neighborhood newspapers and magazines, such as *Rolling Stone*, that were likely be read by young women who would respond to the ads' message. Before long, PREGNANT? CALL COLLECT IN CONFIDENCE, in bold black-and-yellow lettering, began appearing on benches, in buses and taxicabs, across railroad trestles, on bumper stickers, even on Burger King tray liners!

To give you some idea of how radical a move this was at the time, let me show you the lengths to which some of the highly respected agencies would go to protect the "confidentiality" of their clients. Not only did they not advertise, they even refused to place their names or other signs outside their buildings which would in any way indicate what they were about.

The rationale for their maintaining such anonymity was that anyone who'd glimpse couples and obviously pregnant single women entering and exiting the building might make an educated guess as to what was going on inside. The agencies called that being discreet. I called it being foolish. My major concern with their "discretion" was that a troubled young woman might walk right by the building that housed the agency and not know there was help for her inside.

In this world of secret adoption, Golden Cradle billboards were bombshells. Adoption traditionalists were up in arms, criticizing the signs and billboards as "tacky" and castigating me as opportunistic.

It's easy to be judgmental when the problem doesn't really hit home to you. I just wonder, though, if the people who criticized the ads were themselves childless or if they had kids who wanted to adopt or who needed to place a child for adoption . . . would they still think the signs were in such poor taste? Or would they view my efforts in a different light?

Another reason for some people's discomfort with the signs is that talking about pregnancy is talking about s-e-x. Some critics think that if you don't talk about it, it doesn't happen. That's nonsense. Golden Cradle billboards are there to educate people to the fact that they do have choices about what to do about an unintended pregnancy. They are there to keep babies from being found in trash cans.

Golden Cradle has also been accused of using its ads to get babies. My answer to that is "Yes—especially the babies who might otherwise be abused or abandoned." We reach out to pregnant women, many of whom don't know where else to turn. If you need help, our billboards are beautiful!

One of the major accomplishments of Golden Cradle *and* those billboards is that we took the mystique out of adoption. We advertised in the Yellow Pages of 168 cities in 21 states. Before 1982, when we successfully pressured the telephone company to run a listing under Adoption Services, nobody had ever done that. (Now everybody's doing it!) We talked about adoption on 65 television shows, 58 radio talk shows, in 15 different magazines and 475 newspapers nationwide.

If I sound like I'm on a soapbox, so be it. For many years, a lot of people hoped that I would slip on that soap and be put out of business. Now some of those same people are standing in line to get up on the box. The bottom line is: we helped people and we got results!

Learning from the Birth Mothers

The second break from tradition was the way that Golden Cradle has always treated birth mothers, as full partners in the adoption process. From the beginning, counseling of these young women has been paramount. Unfortunately, my first experience in working with a birth mother was brief and very disappointing. Luckily, it was not a precursor of things to come.

In early December, 1979, about two weeks after meeting the Wagners, I received a phone call from a young woman who had seen one of the ads I had placed in a local paper. "I'm pregnant," she told me, "and I want to place my baby."

Instead of asking her to come down to the warehouse, I suggested that we meet in a public place like a restaurant or bowling alley—someplace where she would feel comfortable. She told me her name, said that there was a diner right down the street from her home, and that's where we met: in the Greiner Diner.

Boy, was I nervous! Again, I needed to come up with a list of questions to fit a situation I'd never before confronted. "How old are you?" I began. "When was the last time you visited your doctor? Have you seen a gynecologist? Do you have your parents' support? What's the situation with the birth father? Is he single? Married? Does he know that you're pregnant?"

The young woman sat facing me, sipping her Coke. She was twenty years old, she replied. She had recently been to a doctor, who confirmed that she was pregnant. Her parents knew about the situation, and she had their support for whatever decision she made. Her mind was made up. She was going to place the baby for adoption. She made it very clear that she did not want to talk about the baby's father.

I offered to find a responsible couple who would adopt the baby, and to see that all the medical and legal expenses were taken care of. I also offered her the opportunity to write letters to the child, leaving off her name and address. They would go through me, I said, and I would forward them to the adoptive couple. Would she mind if the couple wanted to write back?

I had not yet become an advocate of the kind of openness in adoption that so many of our birth parents and adopting couples are comfortable with today (and that I now wish existed between our family and Josh's birth mother), but somewhere inside me was the feeling that I wanted to personalize adoption in some way. I mean, transferring a child isn't the same as providing you with the set of jumper cables that you need for your car. I give them to you and you keep them. There's no feeling for that set of jumper cables. A child, a human being, is something else.

The birth mother said, "It sounds nice." And that she'd get back to me.

I waited . . . and when I didn't hear from her, I called. She had decided to place the baby through an attorney, she said. He, too, had offered to cover all of her expenses. He'd also offered her ten thousand dollars in cash. I don't mind losing fair and square, but this *wasn't* fair. I wished her good luck, but I remember feeling very angry. (I also wondered how much money the adopting couple would have to come up with, how much the attorney would be making on the deal.)

You lose some and you win some. Within a month or so, I had heard from several birth mothers who were willing to work with me. I was flabbergasted. There'd been so many years when Weezie and I had struggled to adopt one child, there'd been so many people who told us there weren't any birth mothers willing to place their babies, and now—in a relatively short time—I'd met and made arrangements to work with several. (This was also before there'd been any publicity about what I was doing. Once the media began covering Golden Cradle, I often found myself interviewing three, four, five birth mothers a day.)

While I felt that I had a pretty good idea of what adoptive parents were all about, when I went into the business of facilitating adoptions I had absolutely no preconceptions about the birth mothers. By the time I found myself interviewing the fourth . . . fifth . . . sixth young woman who was struggling to reach a decision about what to do with an unplanned pregnancy, I had a much better understanding of some of their anxieties. They were concerned about medical bills. They were concerned about how they were going to feel afterward. Some of the questions I could answer. Some of them I couldn't.

I was concerned about their support system . . . that whatever their decision was, they had the support of their parents . . . that they wouldn't be crucified. Having been a phys-ed teacher and a Big Brother, knowing kids . . . all of that helped me a lot. But it was mostly on-the-job training. I listened real good.

Some of the birth mothers were married and (as in the case of the young woman who placed her baby with the Wagners) could not accommodate another child. Others were married and pregnant by their boyfriends. Of the unmarried women, a great many were the youngest children in families where there were many children. Many came from families where there was alcoholism or abuse.

If they said to me, "My parents don't know," I usually suggested to them—not right off the bat, but during a second meeting—that they tell their parents. They said, "My parents will kill me." I heard that all the time. I said, "Get your mother aside, toward the end of the week when she's relaxed and looking forward to the weekend. Take her hand in yours, look her in the eye, and tell her, 'Mom, I'm pregnant. I'm going to need your support.'"

They'd ask, "What about my father?"

I'd tell them, "You and your mother decide that. My personal feeling is that you ought to be honest, but I don't know your particular situation." I also told them, "You have to tell the birth father, too."

Solving the Housing Problem

Another frequent concern of the birth mothers was finding a place to stay. For a variety of reasons, several decided to leave their communities while awaiting the birth of their babies. Others found the decision made for them by parents who were angry, or disappointed, or concerned about the effects of the pregnancy on other children in the home. Some of the women had to leave their jobs and could no longer afford to maintain a place to live.

I kept thinking, *maternity home, maternity home*, but most maternity homes went out with high-button shoes. I knew that there were still some maternity homes run by religious orders, but they had a particular orientation and, I'd been told by some of the women who'd spent time there, they were not strong on helping the residents to consider their choices and deal with the aftermath of their decisions. If I was to help the birth mothers, I needed to be able to meet their housing needs in some humane and affordable fashion.

The solution, once I hit upon it, seemed both simple and right. It still does. But it continues to evoke controversy in some quarters to this very day. I thought: why not ask adoptive applicants to house an expectant mother—making certain that these applicants would not be the people to adopt her child. (That could be too close for comfort.) I reasoned that this would help each side see the other as flesh and blood. It would give the birth mother a better feeling for the kind of home and people her baby would go to. It would also provide the host family with a greater appreciation for the young women who have reached the decision to place their babies, and an understanding of the reasons for that choice. In other words, the two principal parties to an adoption decision would get to see the flip side of the coin.

Again, no money changed hands. The adoptive applicants volunteered to house the birth mothers. During those early years, Weezie and I also opened our home to more than a dozen young women who needed a place to stay. One summer we had three expectant mothers living in our home. They'd come from Texas, North Carolina, and Vermont.

People criticized the housing program on the grounds that the mothers-to-be would be coerced by the adoptive applicants with whom they lived into making a plan to place their babies. The statistics on placement provide the best answer to that accusation. Of the expectant mothers who elected to use our housing program, 40 percent did not go through with adoption. Most of these women decided to keep their babies. Of the 253 babies who were placed through the program in the first three and a half years, only eight birth mothers later changed their minds. A very small percentage chose abortion as a response to an unintended pregnancy.

In all the years of running this program, we have had very few problems—and none of a serious nature. One young woman entertained her boyfriend when the husband and wife were out for the evening—and without their permission. She was dropped from the program. But another young birth mother grew so close to the host family that she lives on in a carriage house on their property four years after she relinquished her baby.

In case you're wondering what the boarding program feels like—from both sides—here is a description from two of its participants.

The Birth Mother's Perspective

Lauren (not her real name) is twenty-three years old. Two months ago, she gave birth to a healthy boy who now lives with his adoptive parents. Lauren currently lives with her mother, while she makes plans for her future. For a while, toward the end of her pregnancy, she lived with a couple we will call SueEllen and Jack. Here, in Lauren's words, is what that experience was like:

> When I found out I was pregnant, it was clear that (for a variety of reasons) adoption was my only alternative. The baby's father was very much in my life—we're still together—but we were not ready for marriage. Babies need more than a lot of love, and that's all I had to give.
>
> I found out about the housing program after I contacted Golden Cradle, but I didn't think I would be taking advantage of it. I had a job, an apartment, and a roommate. But then I had a falling-out with my roommate, and I *had* to move. To be honest, the way that I looked at the housing program then was that it would offer me a few months of rent-free living. So I accepted the agency's offer of a place to stay for three to four months, until my baby was born.
>
> I was nervous when I moved in with SueEllen and Jack, not because I was afraid that we wouldn't get along (I'm a pretty easygoing person) but because of the feelings that anyone would have who found themselves in the situation of moving in with somebody you didn't know, and so you wouldn't feel real comfortable. After three days, I felt as if I'd known SueEllen and Jack all my life. For one thing, it turned out that we had so many things in common. Jack was into sports, and I like football. SueEllen and I would talk about our jobs, our feelings, and we were so much alike. We went to the store together to shop for groceries. The three of us had dinner together. It felt like family.
>
> We got so close that I even asked SueEllen if she would like to be in the delivery room with me. She said that she'd be honored. And that made me feel good. We practiced different routes from her home to the hospital. When the time came, SueEllen drove me to the hospital and stayed with me through the whole labor process and birth.
>
> Living with SueEllen and Jack, I learned so much. I didn't know much about adoption before, but being with them I realized how happy I was going to make somebody, and that made me feel much better. Before, I knew I was making the right decision for the baby. Now, I also knew that I was doing something special for some other people as well.

I also think that it was good for SueEllen and Jack to hear my side of the story. We keep in touch and I know that, when they get their baby—whether or not they get to meet the birth mother—they will have a better understanding of how and why people are able to make this very difficult decision.

The Housing Couple's Story: Two Different Experiences

A couple I'll call Angie and Tim are the adoptive parents of a beautiful three-year-old daughter. While in the process of adopting, the couple served as a host family to two different birth mothers—and had two very different experiences. Angie tells the story:

> We weren't certain, at first, about whether we wanted to work with Golden Cradle because I wasn't sure about wanting to be involved in the housing program. I had a real distorted picture of the birth mothers—that they were drug addicts or in some other way troubled or disreputable. Eventually (to be honest, a little reluctantly), Tim and I agreed to serve as a host family.
>
> When the actual request came, however, I wasn't ready. The agency called me at work to say that there was a thirty-year-old expectant mother (I'll call her Melissa) who needed a place to live *that afternoon*. I rushed home from work and set the guest room up. When Melissa arrived, it was awkward. I wanted her to feel at home, but I didn't want to be overly friendly. I didn't know what our relationship was supposed to be.
>
> Melissa was very secretive about the father of her baby. She was also very depressed. One day, she took her anger out on our dog, letting him get soaked after I'd left him in her care and expressly asked her to make sure that he stayed away from the pool—he wasn't supposed to get wet. The second or third night she was with us, she cried all night. That caused *me* to become depressed. I almost felt like Golden Cradle was baby-stealing, that Tim and I might be getting a baby from someone who, like Melissa, seemed so desperately to want to keep her child.

One day, after visiting her doctor, Melissa simply got into her car and drove away. I was really concerned and phoned the agency. Three counselors came over and spoke to Melissa when she returned home. They decided that she wasn't emotionally ready to make a decision to place the baby once it was born, and referred her to another program that would help her with her medical expenses and enable her to keep the baby. That's when I knew that a baby would not be placed with us unless the birth parents decided it was the right decision for the baby *and* for them. That made me feel a lot better. On July 31, we received a letter from Melissa, informing us that she'd delivered a healthy baby on the 17th and thanking us for our help. We later learned that, after spending a few weeks with her infant, she placed the baby privately.

After Melissa left our home, our social worker, Sue, told us, "I promise you a better experience the next time." The *next* time? We didn't have to wait long. On August 1, Sue called about a seventeen-year-old (whom I'll call Sandy) who wanted to go into housing, but was leery. Would I call and speak to her parents?

I was leery too, but I made the call. Sandy's parents wanted to know if we'd be open to having them visit their daughter. We agreed. Would we consent to driving her back home if she became homesick? We said yes. They then asked if I'd be willing to be her birth coach and be in the delivery room with her. When you go through the Golden Cradle program, they tell you that some of the mothers may want you to coach them through delivery. Sometimes, both husband and wife participate; at other times, only one may be involved. You don't have to agree to do this. In one of the better decisions of my life, I said yes.

Sandy lived with us for five weeks—and she was a delight. Since I expected that Tim and I would soon be hearing good news from the agency, I quit my job because it entailed a lot of traveling. As a result, Sandy and I were able to spend a lot of time together. Discovering that we both liked movies, most days we would go down to a video store and select our evening's entertainment. On some weekends, her boyfriend would come down from college and stay with us too. He was pretty supportive of Sandy, but he was scared—afraid that his parents would find out that he'd fathered a child.

It was four in the morning when Sandy's water broke and we rushed her to the hospital. Sandy's contractions were four minutes apart. We did the breathing exercises together. Within thirty-five minutes, I watched as she was delivered of her child: a healthy baby boy. I felt as if I'd witnessed a miracle. I said to Sandy, "Why don't you call the birth father?" Then I placed the call for her, and went out of the room.

I was holding this beautiful infant who, I knew, would soon be going to live with another couple, and I felt happy. It made everything more real. I knew that soon there would be a baby who was destined for us. It was six in the morning. I took out my portable phone and called everybody I knew to tell them what it was like to see a baby born. It was such a privilege, such a neat experience.

Sandy stayed with us for a few days after leaving the hospital. One week later, we received a call from the agency announcing the arrival of our daughter. I could go on forever about how special this little girl is, about the incredible experience of having her in our lives. In fact, I'm even glad I was infertile. Otherwise, I often think, I wouldn't have my daughter. Adoption has been wonderful. For me, knowing Sandy and seeing her baby born was simply the cherry on the cake.

About the idea of coaching a birth mother through labor and delivery: I should make it clear that this is absolutely not required, but that it can be a very special experience (for those who are given the opportunity to assist in a birth and who accept it). I know. In the first three years of Golden Cradle's operation, I helped in the delivery of more than forty babies. Either the birth mothers didn't want their families to know about the pregnancy, or they felt that it would be too emotional an experience for their parents, or they were simply alone in a strange city. Whatever the reason, they wanted someone to be with them, and I was there. The first time I watched a birth mother deliver, it was a miracle. It always is.

Facing Different Kinds of Pressure

I thought I had a good understanding of adoptive applicants, having been one myself, but even here I had a lot to learn. The first year, I placed fifteen babies. I turned away only one couple. On paper, everything about them looked good—length of marriage, professions, standing in the community. I couldn't put my finger on what was wrong, but they just didn't seem warm. They weren't "together" in the way you expect couples to be in a situation like this. After a few meetings, I felt the need to tell them, "I don't know if I'm going to be able to work with you." That day, I got a phone call from the woman's mother who offered me five thousand dollars if I would place a baby with the couple. Boy, did that turn me off. Within a year, I heard that they were divorced.

I was offered money four times in the early years. Once, the offer was made by the agent of a major television personality. The way he put it was, "We're prepared to make a thirty-thousand-dollar contribution to you." I said, "If I hear the word money or contribution again, I'm going to hang up." (Don't get me wrong: I welcome contributions to Golden Cradle—we're a nonprofit organization and we *need* contributions in order to exist and continue to do our work—but we won't accept money as a bribe. That just doesn't wash.)

Another time, the wife of a prominent politician tried to pressure me into giving priority to her adoption application. I told her that I didn't play favorites, that I treated everyone equally. After a while, the word gets around. People know that they're dealing with a straight shooter, and they respect that.

And everywhere I turned there were *lots* of people to deal with. First of all, at home there was my growing family. You've heard the old saying, "Adopt and you'll get pregnant"? Well, I don't believe that's any reason for adopting, but it sure as heck happened in our case. It was certainly unexpected, and it was fast. Just seven weeks after Josh arrived, Weezie conceived. And on August 18, 1980, our daughter Abby was born. Our two children are ten months apart in age.

I regret to admit that of all the demands on my time and attention, it was this family—the one I'd waited so long to achieve—that got the least of both. It hurts to look back at what I was like during those years. In short, I was a lousy husband and a lousy father. But I was becoming very successful in the other areas of my life. Almost in spite of the fact that most of my attention was elsewhere, the auto supply business was doing well. Very well. I had to add space and staff to keep up with its growth.

At the same time, Golden Cradle was growing too. In September 1980, I felt secure enough about the program to register its name. At first, the adoption practice took up file space in my office, but it quickly spilled over into rooms that had been built to house other business projects I'd hoped to become involved in. Well, they'd just have to wait.

It seemed that I was constantly on the phone. My secretary, Mary, once counted it up. I averaged 105 phone calls a day, 80 percent of them dealing with Golden Cradle. I had to get a pad for my ear.

I was a schizo. One minute I'd be berating a salesman for late delivery. The next minute, the phone would ring and there'd be a birth mother on the other end of the line. My tone would change as I'd answer, "Golden Cradle. How can I help you?" It was always, "How can I help you? What can I do for you?" We'd talk for a while, make an appointment to meet, and say good-bye. Then I'd go back to dressing down the salesman. Golden Cradle was a mix of common sense and passion. It took its toll on me and on my marriage. As anyone who knew me in those days can tell you, I was obsessed. Angelo Pinto was there when it all began, and he remembers it well:

> I was a manufacturer's rep in those days and Arty was one of my customers. I remember when he moved the automotive business from the old building into the new warehouse, and I can tell you that things were hectic. From my point of view, when he started to become more involved with Golden Cradle, getting through a business meeting with him became even more difficult. You'd be in his office, waiting to go over the merchandise that he was ordering, and he was on the telephone. "Okay" . . . "We can help you" . . . "We'll put your name on the list" . . . "You got it" . . . "I'll try to help you." So you'd be in his office for an hour, and you got fifteen minutes of his time. The other forty-five minutes were Golden Cradle's.
>
> You had to be there at the time to see this place. I remember young girls would come in here, and Arty would help them. Couples would come in with babies, and he'd get

down on the floor to play with the babies. One of the rooms was filled with donations: baby clothes, cribs, strollers, playpens. Volunteers would come in; salesmen and secretaries would come in. It really *was* hectic. But Arty is very organized, and somehow he would know which of the many papers that were strewn about on his desk or on the floor was the one that you needed. Somehow everything got done.

Growth of a Cottage Industry into an Agency

I started getting more and more phone calls, and I couldn't run from one end of the state to another, so I asked the birth mothers if they would mind coming in to see me at the warehouse, explaining to them that I was an adoptive father and trying to run Golden Cradle and a business at the same time. In the three and a half years that the agency was run out of the warehouse, only two or three birth mothers failed to show up of the 440 with whom I made appointments to meet.

The greater Golden Cradle's success, the more I was an embarrassment to the social service system. They chided me for not having the appropriate credentials to do social work. My retort to that is that I stop for people on the highway to help get their car started. I carry extra antifreeze. I carry a universal fan belt. The people I help don't check to see if I'm a licensed mechanic. They're happy to accept my help. If I came up with ideas to solve some of the problems in the social service system, they could have learned from me. If I made some mistakes, they could still have welcomed me and helped me to correct them.

They criticized me for not doing home studies. After the first year, I did do home studies. I hired a social worker who would do home studies on Golden Cradle couples that were far more complete than the fifty-five-minute interview Weezie and I had experienced with Gladney. What's more, Golden Cradle required that the home studies be completed *before* couples were accepted into the program.

If this were a video, here's where I'd move it fast forward—first to June 1983, when you'd see Golden Cradle being moved out of the warehouse and into its own offices in Bala-Cynwyd, Pennsylvania, and then to June of 1987, when the agency was relocated to its present quarters on the eighth floor of the Executive Office Building in Cherry Hill, New Jersey. (You'd also see dedicated volunteers carrying files, boxes, desks, teddy bears, and maternity clothes from one location to another, as well as painting the rooms and papering the walls. Thank God for our volunteers!)

Although the agency remains reliant on the continuing assistance of its many volunteers and supporters, Golden Cradle is now a highly professional operation—a New Jersey-licensed, nonprofit and nonsectarian organization with an annual budget of well over a million dollars, an outstandingly capable executive director, Marlene Piasecki, and a paid staff of eighteen full and part-time employees.

If asked to briefly summarize our philosophy, I would do it in two sentences: (1) The child is the primary client; (2) Our focus is on families. Because we want to achieve what is best for the child, we strive to assist birth parents and childless couples alike in deciding whether adoption is right for them.

Over the years, adoption has changed in many ways, often prodding us to change with it. Today, for example, the birth mother is a more educated consumer. There are many choices open to her. We have to provide a service that best meets her wishes and her needs. We have also to support the adoptive parents as they consider these changes (especially toward greater openness) and reevaluate the feelings they may have had about privacy and exclusivity. *And* we have an obligation to educate the community so that they can grow with us, seeing adoption as a healthful response to the situation of children needing families.

All of this, I think, has been to the good. At Golden Cradle, we have gained a much greater understanding of adoption's reality: that the baby does not come from an agency (or from a lawyer, or from any other intermediary), but from a birth parent, and that, following placement, the baby will no longer be the responsibility of the agency but of the adoptive parents. That recognition has served to change our practice so that, increasingly, we see our role as a facilitator, leaving the decision making (as much as possible) to the parties who are most vitally involved.

Sure, I can hear you saying as you read this, that sounds pretty impressive, but the reality is that Golden Cradle (like all agencies) *does* make Solomonic decisions every day—if only because it accepts just so many applicants and turns many others away. That's true. It's impossible for our agency, for *any* agency engaged in facilitating adoptions in this day and age, to satisfy the many requests for adoptable babies. In 1989 (the last year for which figures are available as I write this), Golden Cradle received over three thousand inquiries from couples hoping to adopt—down by 40 percent from the preceding year only because we put a halt, for several months, on accepting applications. About a hundred couples were then invited to participate in groups for prospective parents, which are opened twice a year.

A look at our placement statistics gives you some idea of why intake is necessarily limited. In 1989, Golden Cradle received 1,900 inquiries from birth parents. Of the 129 who entered Golden Cradle's Options Counseling Program, 58 chose adoption for their infants. The others decided to assume the responsibility of parenting their children. Given the large discrepancy between the many people wishing to adopt and the relatively few babies who are made available for adoption, we have had to set certain criteria for the couples we will work with. They must be married at least three years, fall between the ages of twenty-five and forty-five, and have documented proof of infertility. For the most part, we have also tried to confine our intake to families living in our general geographic area (New Jersey, Philadelphia, and Wilmington, Delaware), where we are better able to serve them.

Here's what we offer to the birth family:

— information about all the options available to the birth mother, birth father, and their unborn child
— pre- and postnatal medical care, including childbirth education classes
— ongoing counseling throughout the pregnancy

- the use of Golden Cradle's birth mother tutoring, housing, and transportation services
- if adoption is the decision, the opportunity to select the adoptive couple from several applicant families and, if desired, to speak or meet with the adoptive family
- the opportunity to receive photographs and letters from the child's adoptive family for six months or for as long as the birth and adoptive parents agree upon
- the opportunity to send correspondence and photographs to the child and the adoptive family through the agency
- the ability to receive counseling and referral services following adoption

And here is what the adoptive applicants we work with can expect:

- counseling and education about all aspects of adoption
- help in achieving an appropriate adoptive placement
- background information and a complete medical history from the child's birth family
- the opportunity to communicate with the birth family through letters and pictures and to choose the degree of openness with which the couple will feel most comfortable, understanding that there must be agreement on this between the adopting couple and the birth parents
- linkups with others in the adoption process who can provide friendship, information, and support
- a baby

Sometimes, it seems to me as if all of this happened in the wink of an eye. At other times, I am well aware that the journey has been long and arduous. Once in a while, even painful. But this great adventure in adoption has never lacked for challenge or excitement. I have learned a lot. And I have gained much more in the special friendships that I've made along the way. And so I find myself still wanting to give back. I can accomplish that, I hope, by reaching out to others—to you—who now stand at the beginning of that all-important journey, wondering which way to go, or whether to venture forward at all.

II

A Candid Look at Adoption and Its Cast of Characters

4

Why You? Confronting Infertility

Doctors classify couples as infertile if they fail to conceive after one year of unprotected intercourse. But if you've been "trying" for a while and getting nowhere, you know that the tension sets in well before the official diagnosis. It's there from the moment you suspect that something which ought to be happening is *not* happening. You're just *not* getting pregnant. Something's wrong.

Unfortunately, you're not alone in dealing with this problem. Infertility is a complex, often baffling medical challenge that affects an estimated 17 percent of married couples in this country alone. Experts have identified a number of likely causes of infertility, including: today's sexual freedom which has led to an increase in sexually transmitted diseases such as gonorrhea and an insidious bacterial infection known as chlamydia; prolonged use of the pill; the devastating effects of various intrauterine devices designed to forestall pregnancy, not foreclose it; and the choice of sterilization to prevent conception—which turns into an infertility problem when the individual, now desirous of having children, seeks to have the operation reversed and is not successful.

Given the fact that more men and women are finding themselves in second marriages and wanting to have children with their new spouses, sterilization reversal is being sought more frequently nowadays in an attempt to achieve conception. The good news here is that new microsurgical techniques make it easier for doctors to reconnect previously cut or tied-off fallopian tubes in women and to reverse vasectomies in men, enabling conception to take place. The bad news? If you're among the estimated 50 percent of people for whom these procedures do not work, you don't need me to tell you what the bad news is.

Rumors of an "Epidemic" Have Been Greatly Exaggerated

Factors like these, plus the tremendous publicity that's being accorded to some of the more high-tech methods of producing a baby, help foster a dangerous general impression that an "epidemic of infertility" is raging across the country. I believe the notion is dangerous because it leads couples to panic the moment they suspect that they may need some help (or some more time) in order to conceive a child, and off they go—running blindly through the infertility-treatment jungle without a guide.

Let's take a look at what's really happening. According to demographer William D. Mosher, the overall percentage of all married couples who are infertile has not changed significantly in recent years. What *has* been happening is that an increasing number of husbands and wives have been delaying childbearing. Women and men are marrying later, then waiting to get their dual careers comfortably off the ground before they decide to start a family. When they do resolve that the time is right, many discover that there's more to having a child than simply making the decision to stop using contraception.

Without question, infertility increases with age, Mosher points out. For example, women over thirty-five are nearly twice as likely to be infertile as women under thirty—and far more anxious when pregnancy doesn't happen right away. In the olden days (really only about a dozen years ago), couples who saw a doctor because they were having trouble conceiving were often told to "relax and give it time." And many had the time to give it. For today's older aspiring parents, however, time is a luxury they can ill afford. Their biological clocks are ticking loudly.

Let's Talk About Feelings

Statistics aside, when the problem of infertility strikes home, the news that a lot of other homes in the neighborhood are similarly devastated doesn't alter its impact. It hurts. For one thing, infertility is hardly a condition that anyone is likely to anticipate developing someday—in the same way, for example, that a person might be wary of coming down with diabetes or developing heart disease because there's a family predisposition to these conditions. But a tendency to infertility? Since none of us arrives on this planet through spontaneous generation, infertility isn't the kind of condition that we're likely to think of as a personal disaster waiting to occur.

And when it does, our first reaction is often *not* to react. I know all about denial. We think: *If I don't talk about infertility, if I refuse to even think about it, maybe it won't be there . . . or maybe it will go away.* I also recall the early silences—those times when husband and wife are wary of saying something accusatory or otherwise hurtful to one another, so they tiptoe around The Problem and keep things in. Just when communication is most important, intimate conversation between the couple becomes impossible. Some partners can get stuck in denial for a long, long time.

Eventually, however, you are going to have to face up to the possibility that there may indeed be some problem—and that it needs to be addressed. Once acknowledged, reality has a way of hitting like a bolt of lightning. The first thing you think is *Why me?* Then *Why us?*, because however and whomever the bolt hits, there's no question that infertility is an issue that is shared by the couple—although physiologically the man or the woman may be identified as the source of the problem. Still, there are individual feelings that must be addressed. Feelings of incompetency. Feelings of frustration. Feelings of guilt. (The feelings of loss come later.)

I know. Like you, I've been there.

I know how hard it can be just to reach a decision to see a doctor because making the appointment is a concrete act that gives life to your suspicions. On the one hand, you want to know if there really *is* a problem. On the other hand, you don't want to have your worst fears confirmed. Compared to taking that first step into a doctor's examining room for a consultation, man's first step on the moon had to have been a piece of cake. (Typically, it is the woman who takes that step into the doctor's office, although infertility doesn't really play favorites. Experts now know that, up to 40 percent of the time, infertility cases involve male problems. In fully 30 percent of couples experiencing infertility, both the man and the woman have problems.)

Accepting that you may have an infertility problem does not mean giving up. On the contrary, it can start you on the journey toward *doing something about it*. Be prepared for what may be an arduous trip.

From my own experience and those of the thousands of infertile couples I have met through my work with Golden Cradle, I know how dehumanizing the workups are that each of you must undergo, how humiliating it feels to have your private life dissected and placed under a microscope for public examination.

I know how disheartening it can feel to go, hopefully, from one doctor to another, without a successful resolution of The Problem. And I know how frustrating it can be when doctors tell you *what* to take but not *why*. When you summon up the courage to ask, they answer only, "It works for some people." I know that in the area of infertility, medicine is more an art than a science.

I know about the loss of control that you feel as you're forced to accept dependence on others—doctors, nurses, lab technicians, go-betweens, social workers, lawyers—in order to achieve what you once thought would be yours as a kind of natural right: a child, a chance to replicate yourself, a family of your own.

I know about mechanical lovemaking. It's the tap on the shoulder at two in the morning after the temperature's been taken: the signal that this is the time To Do It. Or receiving a message in the office—the thermometer says now!—and driving home over icy roads at breakneck speed.

I know about the other kinds of tensions that infertility treatments can produce. "I took Clomid for one month," I remember being told by one woman, "and every morning I woke up to face the personality of the day. One day, I was weepy; the next a screaming shrew. My husband was afraid to come home because he didn't know which one of me would meet him at the door." No one had warned the couple that extreme mood changes were one of Clomid's possible side effects.

I know how infertility can lead you to feel guilty about letting down your own parents because, somehow, you failed by not making them grandparents.

I know the feelings that well up in you when a well-meaning relative suggests glibly, "Why don't you just relax" or "Why don't the two of you go on a vacation?" As if all that stands in the way of having a baby is your own anxiety.

And since we're talking about others' insensitivity, here's a new put-down that today's infertile couples tell me they are being made to confront: being labeled a Yuppie or DINK (Double Income, No Kids) by others, which translates into criticism of the couple for being selfish and implicitly suggests that their childlessness is a matter of choice.

I know that, for a time, infertility can color your whole life, making it hard to attend family reunions, a baby shower for a friend, or even to walk down the aisles of a supermarket. Inevitably, you're going to have to pass the shelves of disposable diapers. Next aisle? That's where the baby foods are stacked. To add further insult, it always happens that there's an obviously pregnant woman, with a small child seated in the front of her shopping cart, heading directly toward you.

I understand depression. While I don't presume to know exactly what it's like for the woman, each and every month, when she gets an unwanted period (I remember one woman telling me that she couldn't go into work two days of every month—she was *that* distressed), I still vividly recall the frustration *I* felt in wanting to be supportive of my wife while struggling, at the same time, to cope with my own feelings of disappointment and inadequacy.

I know that infertility can really take its toll on man and wife—as individuals and as a couple. I also am convinced that it's important, when you start on the journey, to take the long view, to keep in mind that things *do* have a way of working out. The experience of a couple whom I'll call Rob and Sharon serves as a case in point.

Rob speaks first:
"Sharon and I had been living together for some time. We married *because* we had made the decision to have children, and we began trying on our honeymoon. After about ten months, Sharon decided to talk to her doctor, who did a medical work-up on her, saw nothing wrong, and then said, 'Why don't you have your husband come in?' When I did, the doctor found that my sperm count was low. *That* was the moment when lightning struck home."

Rob was referred to a urologist who recommended surgery to repair a varicocele. The majority of men with varicoceles are fertile when they are young, but their fertility gradually declines. Rob, by then in his mid-thirties, found the operation more psychologically than physically painful. "Everyone I came into contact with at the hospital, everyone I opened up to, required me to say, 'I have a fertility problem,' " he explains. "And each time was as embarrassing as the first."

Following the operation, Rob was given a series of hormonal injections, which he also found humiliating: "Whenever I went to the lab, there would be a different nurse asking loudly, 'What are the shots for?' I was close to tears. I'm a sensitive man, and I didn't realize that the feelings of inadequacy brought on by infertility could go so deep—at least they did for me. My self-esteem was shattered. Infertility invaded everything in my life—my marriage, my friendships, my work. I wasn't a happy person."

Rob's comments provide a fairly typical description of the feelings experienced by many men in this situation. Let's listen now to how Sharon, his wife, recalls this period in their lives:

"It was very difficult. Rob doesn't verbalize his feelings. I knew he was hurting—so was I—but I felt shut out. Through all this, though, I didn't lose hope that we'd be able to conceive. While Rob was going through the various procedures to improve his sperm count, I dutifully continued to make the rounds of doctors . . . many doctors. At some point, one of them discovered that I had a severe case of endometriosis [a condition in which the endometrium tissue lining the uterus grows abnormally outside the uterus in other portions of the abdominal cavity], which is a common cause of infertility problems in women. So, like Rob, I also had surgery and still failed to get a baby going.

"At another point, I was taking fertility drugs to spur ovulation. We also tried artificial insemination by donor [AID], arguing that half of our genes would be better than none. To be honest, I think another reason that we went for AID was so that, if we did have a baby, nobody would have to know that it wasn't genetically connected to both of us.

"It's hard to explain," she continues, "but all the while that we were trying different drugs and medications *and* going in and out of hospitals in order to have a child, we still were unable to confide in people (even our families) that there was a problem. We were too embarrassed to let people know. They believed that we just didn't want to have children. The worst part of it all, I think, were the silences—not letting others in on what we were experiencing, not letting one another in on what we were feeling."

We do a lot of talking about infertility at the meetings we hold with adoptive applicants at Golden Cradle, and this elicits two typical reactions. The first is, "Do we *have* to talk about it here? We've been through so much already." The second (and more prevalent) reaction is, "What a relief!"

For some couples, you see, the first group meeting at the agency is also their first opportunity to speak with others who are experiencing infertility. This can be very relieving. "That meeting was a turning point for us," says Sharon. "You can't imagine what it means to walk into a room full of people with experiences just like yours . . . being able to talk . . . even laugh . . . about a subject you couldn't even bring yourself to mention aloud before you entered that room. For the first time since we got on the infertility merry-go-round, Rob and I no longer felt so alone."

It is the passage of time that has made it possible for Rob and Sharon to now speak eloquently about what once was unspeakable. Time—and the two little children, a son and a daughter, whose photographs they carry in their wallets and will show off at the drop of a hat. Rob and Sharon gained a family through adoption. They have come a long way, and *that's* what I hope you will take with you from their story—that even when things seem bleakest, you have got to hold on to the fact that you *will* move beyond the difficult periods, and that good things *can* happen to good people.

Let's Talk About Options, Too

I feel strongly that every agency, lawyer, or other intermediary to whom couples turn for assistance in adopting has an obligation to do some work with them on infertility. I also believe that couples have an obligation to themselves, to find out as much as they can, as soon as they can, because so much is available nowadays to treat infertility. According to the American Fertility Society, 70 percent of couples can be helped by current treatments.

While I don't think it's necessary or even desirable to go around announcing to all and sundry that you're having a hard time making a baby (in the same way that I do encourage people to tell everybody when they're looking to adopt), I'm convinced that it *is* important to meet and talk with others who are also struggling with infertility. Joining Resolve, the national organization providing medical information and emotional support for couples and individuals with fertility problems, is a step that ought to be taken early on.

Nowadays, when there are so many different procedures and products for the infertile couple to consider, becoming an informed consumer is more important than ever before. Resolve can be very helpful in suggesting doctors and specialists who are knowledgeable about infertility matters, including the many subspecialties that fall under that ungainly umbrella. It is important for you to be involved in your own treatment. The more you know, the better you will be able to make decisions about the course of action that seems best for you as individuals and as a couple.

In the early days of Golden Cradle, back when it was essentially a one-man operation, I would advise couples to hold off on pursuing adoption until they had done "everything possible" to conceive. (Among other things, I reasoned that a successful conception makes two families happy: the one that will have their baby born to them and the other who will adopt the baby that might have been earmarked for couple number one.) I still feel this way, except that today's advances in reproductive technology give new meaning to the phrase "everything possible."

Suddenly, it seems as if just about anything is possible—from *gamete intrafallopian transfer* (GIFT), in which eggs and sperm are combined outside of the body and immediately placed in the fallopian tubes to achieve fertilization, to *in vitro fertilization*, where fertilization takes place outside of the body in a laboratory; from *surrogate arrangements* in which a birth mother contracts to be artificially inseminated with the father's sperm, to *gestational surrogacy*, where a fetus is conceived in a test tube before being implanted into the uterus of the surrogate mother. Depending on how you look at it, it's either a brave new world that you're stepping into or a mine field.

High-tech infertility treatment has created new emotional struggles because each new technique is tempting. For many couples, infertility treatment becomes an obsession, turning otherwise intelligent, capable people into treatment addicts. Each time they come close to calling a halt, there is a new medication, a new drug, a new procedure, holding out the tantalizing possibility that conception just might be possible.

While the upside of all of this is increased hope and help for couples struggling with infertility, the downside is provided by the unhappy reality that the success rate for certain of these procedures is *not* reassuring. Congressional hearings held in 1989 revealed that only about 9 percent of women who undergo in vitro fertilization treatments have a baby as a result. Further, the results of a recent government investigation into 169 centers offering in vitro services found that less than half had produced a single successful pregnancy.

Adding to the couple's stress is the fact that treatments for infertility do not come cheap. The infertility business has become a multibillion-dollar industry. Insurance may cover some, but not all, of the procedures, and it is not unusual for couples to beg, borrow, and mortgage the house in endless attempts to produce a baby to occupy it.

All of the above explains why I no longer find myself giving people advice to do "everything possible" to conceive before they consider adoption. Instead, I suggest doing *everything reasonable* to conceive. This has become an important distinction.

The definition of what is "reasonable," however, differs from couple to couple and even from husband to wife within each twosome. Lyn and Jack, for example, continued to try for ten years, during which time Lyn had a laparoscopy, took fertility drugs, underwent two attempts at artificial insemination, experienced three miscarriages, and finally managed to achieve a successful pregnancy (six months of which was spent lying on her back, gazing up at the bedroom ceiling). As Lyn now looks down at her infant daughter gurgling happily in her crib, she says triumphantly, "And to think that the doctors told us that we wouldn't be able to have children!"

For Lyn and Jack, ten years was a reasonable wait. For Beverly and Curt, however, the effort to adopt began as soon as they were diagnosed as having an infertility problem. Beverly explains: "We didn't want to waste time in pursuing treatments of dubious value that could better be spent in raising a child. The bottom line for us was parenting. That was far more important than passing along our genes or the way in which a child happened to enter our family."

Resolving Infertility

There comes a time (and it can differ for each of the partners within a marriage as well as from one couple to another) when husband and wife must come together to resolve their feelings about their inability to produce a biological child so they can move on with their lives. Here's what resolution means.

In the heart and mind of each partner, there lives a fantasized child. A son who will grow up to be "the spittin' image of his dad." A daughter who will be a miniature version of her mother. A child who will combine the best features and talents of both parents. Someone who will carry on the line. Resolving infertility requires a couple to grieve, to mourn the loss of their unborn biological child. It means letting go of the fantasy. Resolving infertility does not mean no longer *wanting* to get pregnant, but it does require acceptance of the fact that this may not be possible.

Dealing with infertility is like being educated in the school of hard knocks. Some couples find the strain on their relationship too difficult and drop out. Others emerge stronger from the experience and go on to "graduate" to other options: to living as a child-free couple (choosing as a conscious decision to remain a family of two); to linking their lives with children as Big Brothers and Sisters or as foster parents; or to pursuing adoption as a means of building a family. Resolving infertility means deciding that you are now ready to choose one of these options.

5

Is Adoption the Answer? Facing Your Feelings and Confronting the Myths

If you're reading this book, more than likely you've reached a point where you're at least *thinking* about adopting, wondering whether this method of forming a family is the answer for you. You may be concerned about a number of things, not the least of which is that, in seeking to adopt a child, you could be stepping into yet another impassable maze, opening yourself up to further disappointment, exchanging one fruitless quest for another.

STOP! If *that* is the reason that keeps you from pursuing adoption, you haven't yet got the message of this book. So let me say it again. If you are a basically sound couple (both physically and emotionally) and you truly want to adopt a child, I believe it *will* happen . . . that you can *make* it happen through knowledge and perseverance. You can do it!

I am not going to tell you, however, that adopting is a cinch. After being prodded and poked physically by infertility specialists, you'd better get ready to be prodded and poked emotionally by adoption professionals. Many of the questions they ask will seem personal and highly intrusive. *Biological parents don't have to go through such scrutiny in order to have a baby,* you may think. It seems unfair.

Perhaps it will help you to look at it this way: forming a family by adoption *is* different from creating a family biologically. Some third party (whether it's an agency employee, doctor, lawyer, or other go-between) has to make an important decision about transferring responsibility for a child's well-being from the birth parents to others who are genetically unrelated to the child. To do so without first looking into the suitability of the adoptive applicants would indeed be unfair—to the birth parents who decided in favor of adoption and, most of all, to the child.

If you are thinking about adopting, it is less important to focus on the questions that others will put to you than to ask some important questions of yourself. Before you go forward with applying to agencies, meeting with lawyers, placing ads in papers, whatever . . . you need to explore your own feelings and fears. Adoption is not a one-size-fits-all solution to everyone's infertility problem. It is important, therefore, to come up with an honest appraisal of whether adoption is a comfortable fit for you. This chapter raises many issues which you'd do well to consider.

Examining Your Motivations and Feelings

Do you want to adopt in the hope that you'll then be more likely to conceive one of your "own"? We've all heard stories of couples who adopted and then, almost immediately, became pregnant. (Indeed, my own family is living proof that this sort of thing can happen.) Nevertheless, the incidence of such "happenings" has been greatly exaggerated. Adopting a child isn't a cure for infertility, nor is it an antidote that will make your regret at being unable to conceive and carry a child to term completely disappear. In essence, the question you must ask yourself is this: What's more important to me—to be pregnant or to be a parent? If your answer is the latter, adoption may be for you.

Do you want to adopt a child to make your partner happier? It is not uncommon for either husband or wife to "go along" with an adoption in order to ease the other's pain of living without children. While this may seem to be a noble act, it is an ill-advised one. Agreeing to have a child (by whatever means) is not something that one partner does *for* another. Adoption has to be a mutual decision. Reaching that decision may require some time and counseling for the couple. I urge you to give it the time. A child's happiness depends on it.

Do you want to adopt to add a member to your team? We sometimes find this motive operating in second marriages, where one of the partners is childless and the other has children from a previous marriage. As one disgruntled stepmother expressed it, "Everything my husband and I do seems always to revolve around *his* children. I want a child so I can have someone on *my* team." At Golden Cradle, we are finding that many of the husbands and wives who apply to adopt are in their second marriages. As with first-married couples, we feel strongly that any decision to adopt should rest solely on whether adopting answers the needs and desires of both husband and wife. Only then is adoption the right answer.

Are you considering adopting in order to strengthen a faltering marriage? Infertility can really do a job on husband and wife: making them feel anxious; causing them to regard sex as a programmed act instead of a passionate and loving expression; making them feel guilty. When people are in pain, their marriages often suffer too. Adoption is not something you can use to bolster a shaky marriage. If you're going through a rough time right now, I strongly advise you to concentrate on improving your relationship first. Once you've re-established a foundation that's strong enough to support a family, *then* it's time to go ahead with adopting.

Do you want to adopt a child in order to fulfill your parents' wish to be grandparents? Pleasing other people, no matter how important they are to you, is not a reason for having a child. It's not your parents who will have to handle the 3 A.M. feedings; they're not the ones who will have to lay down the rules about chores or (later) curfews. In short, any children you have will be *your* responsibility. Is it a responsibility that you wish (or are ready) to assume?

Is your extended family supportive of your efforts to adopt? Having sounded a note of caution against expecting your parents to assume responsibility in raising the children, I also want to make the point that you can (and should) expect your parents to be involved in various positive ways, from encouraging your adoption plan to being supportive of the children who join your family when your efforts succeed. Do you suspect that either set of grandparents is likely to differentiate between an adopted grandchild and other grandchildren who are biologically connected to them? If so, don't just wonder about your parents' reactions. Talk to them about their feelings. You're likely to find that your fears are unrealized. But what if you're right? It's important to consider how strong an influence the grandparents *and* their reactions will have on you and any children you adopt.

Can you accept and fully love an adopted child? Having lived so long with the image of the son or daughter whom you hoped to bear, you may be concerned about your ability to love a child who does not fit that cherished picture. I believe it is helpful to give voice to that concern, and then to explore how important it is for you to replicate yourself.

You cannot do that through adoption. At Golden Cradle, we listen carefully to the expectations that are expressed by adoptive applicants. In one case that comes quickly to mind, a couple wanted to be *assured* that the child we would place with them would have the exact same background as theirs. They wanted us to guarantee that the child would be "perfect." (We cannot do that—no more than any obstetrician can assure the parents that any baby born to them will be without flaws *or* that a biological child will live up to the parents' fondest dreams.) We encouraged the couple to drop out of the program, and they did.

People who become adoptive parents must be able to accept "difference." Although some children do bear an uncanny resemblance to their adoptive parents, the likelihood is good that the child will *not* look like you, and that he or she will also have different abilities and personality traits than those that you've seen in your biological family.

There is no way of knowing beforehand just how you will respond to these differences. If you are having doubts along these lines, it may help to raise them candidly with couples who have adopted children. From my own experience and those of the many adoptive parents I have met, I *can* tell you that each of us is convinced that the child we were given is "the best of the bunch." I have little question that every adoptive parent will confirm having felt this way: this child was destined to be ours.

Now consider the following:
Are you comfortable with the idea of raising a child who was not born to you?
Visualize this scene. You're standing in line at the supermarket and the woman behind you comments on your little girl's copper ringlets, which contrast sharply with your own brown hair that hangs straight to your shoulders. "Who ever gave her those beautiful red curls?" the woman remarks while nudging her shopping cart into your leg. Do you squirm, believing that the entire check-out line now knows your secret? Do you blurt out, "She's adopted"? Or can you see yourself being quite comfortable with the difference in appearance? (By the way, people are forever commenting on my son Josh's blond hair and blue eyes. I just tell them, "He got them from his mother." And he did.)

Are you able to picture yourself as the parent of a child whose talents and demeanor may be very different from yours—say, for example, a youngster who would rather play the piano than join the family in touch football, or an outgoing kid in an introverted family? Will you be likely to see the child's positive qualities as a reflection of your influence while attributing any negative characteristics to his or her genetic heritage? If you think you may have trouble accepting a child *without being judgmental,* adoption may not be right for you.

Can you be comfortable with the fact that your child has another set of parents? If you decide to pursue adoption, this may become a very practical question as you decide on the degree of openness in adoption that you can comfortably accept. But openness is not the issue being addressed here. I'm talking, instead, about how you might react to others' reminders (some subtle, some obvious) that your child is adopted. "Do you know anything about her *real* parents?" an inquisitive neighbor may ask, and you'll know she doesn't mean you and your husband. Do you think you'll be able to handle such comments in a way that lets the neighbor know that you are comfortable in your role and able also to acknowledge the existence of the birth parents?

Secondly, do you think you will be comfortable in answering your child's questions about adoption? Right now, I know, your thoughts and hopes are centered on the idea of acquiring a baby, finally, to love and to cherish. But babies grow up. Adoption is a lifelong process.

It is also a different way of building a family—not better, not worse, but certainly different. Over the years, you will find yourselves dealing with certain issues that are unique to the adoptive experience. Several good books have been written on the challenges that arise in raising an adopted child. I recommend that you do some reading now, even before you apply to adopt, and think about how you might respond to some of the special situations—like explaining to your four-year-old that he didn't grow in your tummy . . . or helping your teenager prepare to meet her birth mother. Today is not too soon for you to begin building a sensitivity to these issues so that you will be more comfortable in handling them once a child is placed in your home.

CONFRONTING THE MYTHS

The secrecy that has long been the foundation for adoption has provided fertile ground for the growth of a number of myths. Let's take a look at some of them.

Myth: There Are No Children Available for Adoption Today. This is the first myth that you're likely to encounter. Here's a typical scenario for how this myth is conveyed. You're at a cocktail party, and you mention that you're thinking about adopting. "But I've heard that there are no children available," says the person to your right as he reaches toward a passing tray of hors d'oeuvres. For most people within earshot, it's an innocent enough statement, a bit of common hearsay—but for the person who has spent years on the infertility circuit going from disappointment to dismay, the comment may be heard as a final negation to parenthood. *We will never have a family*, you think. *I'd better just give up.*

The myth is also harmful to the children who *wait* to be adopted, since it virtually denies their existence and keeps many people from considering becoming parents to youngsters who are no longer infants; or those who are not white; or children who need help in dealing with physical, mental, or emotional problems. Yes, there *are* children available for adoption—over thirty-one thousand in America alone, it has been estimated. And, yes, there are also healthy infants who are relinquished for adoption. Whatever your image of "family" is—whether it includes a baby, an older child, or a youngster who could particularly benefit from special care—don't let this myth deter you from pursuing your goal.

Myth: Abortion Is Responsible for the Current "Shortage" of Adoptable Babies. The fact is that the number of births to unmarried mothers has risen dramatically over the past decade. In 1988, the latest year for which figures are available, for example, more than a million babies were born to unmarried mothers in this country, an increase over the preceding year of more than seventy thousand. Furthermore, the vast majority (94 percent) of unmarried women who make the choice to have their babies also elect to raise them. Society has become much more tolerant of unmarried parents and their babies.

Myth: Unwed Mothers Are Pressured into Relinquishing Their Babies. This, too, is largely untrue. I'm not saying that it never happens. Like you, I have read about cases where a birth mother claims that she has been coerced into going ahead with an adoption plan. But I also know of cases where a young woman enters the obstetrics ward having fully decided to place the newborn infant with an adoptive family, only to be chastised by a "well-meaning" nurse who tells her, "You don't mean to tell me that you're going to give that darling little baby away." And the infant is brought to the birth mother's bedside time and again, often against her expressed wishes, until she relents and takes the baby home.

The word "pressure" is not in my vocabulary. At Golden Cradle, we deal in options. I believe that it's important to support the birth parents' decision—either to keep or place their baby—and to provide them with proper information about the alternatives that are available.

Myth: The Adoptee Is a Chosen Child. Fortunately, this myth is going out of fashion. It is a myth that was created by adoptive parents who told their children, "Other parents have to accept whatever child is born to them, but we *chose* you." The myth was supposed to reassure the adopted child that not only is adoption as good as a biologically formed relationship, it is superior to it. I suspect that this myth was created to provide reassurance to the adoptive parents as well.

The reality, of course, is that the adoptive parents wanted a child, the adopted child was in need of a home, and the birth parents needed the assurance that the child they created would be cherished and well cared for. Adoption is a wonderful way to have all these needs met. The reality is far more satisfying than the myth.

Myth: The Birth Parents Were Too Poor to Provide for a Baby. Many of the birth parents we see are middle class.

Myth: The Birth Parents Were Very Young. "They were so young," adoptive parents tell their child, "that they weren't able to provide for your needs or take proper care of you." The parents like this myth because it makes it easier for them to explain the reasons for the child's being placed with them. (It's a variation on the story that both parents died in a car crash.

People who grew up having *this* story told to them say that they often wondered, "But didn't I have any grandparents? Weren't there aunts and uncles who were willing to take me in?")

Today, with the increasing emphasis on openness, it is harder for parents to invent stories about a child's origins. Even when there is some hard-to-take information included in a youngster's history, at some point it will have to be conveyed. At Golden Cradle, we inform our adoptive parents that it's quite reasonable to expect that the child will someday meet the birth parents. If the youngster then learns that he or she has been given misinformation by the adoptive parents, it could have a negative effect on their relationship.

Oh, yes, I forgot to tell you the truth about the age of the birth parents. At Golden Cradle, the age range of our birth mothers goes from thirteen to forty-two. The average age is twenty.

Myth: You Can Never Love an Adopted Child as Your Own. I don't want to be a Pollyanna about this, but I have two children. Josh came to us by adoption, Abby by birth. There is no question that, in the way that parents feel pride and responsibility toward their children, they are both "my own." And don't get me started talking about *love*. I could go on for hours telling you stories about the two greatest kids in the world who, coincidentally, just happen to be mine.

Myth: "He Must Have Got His Terrible Temper from His Birth Parents." That could be true. The birth parents may also be responsible for your little boy's genius at math. What's true is that adopted kids are a mix of good traits and others that are not so admirable. Some of their aptitudes and actions (both good and bad) are part of the baggage that they carry with them from birth. That true for *all* kids. And some (both bad and good) are products of the way we bring them up and what they are exposed to outside of the home environment.

Myth: Adopt and You Ask for Trouble. Certain recent studies do indicate that adoptees may go through some difficult periods while growing up—especially during their adolescence. Adopted children appear to be disproportionately represented among patients in child or family therapy and among adolescents in residential psychiatric facilities. The incidence of learning disabilities among the adopted population has also been found to be higher than in the general population.

Various explanations have been put forward to explain these findings. It's possible, for example, that adoptive parents (who are overwhelmingly middle class) are more likely to seek professional help for their children and themselves in times of crisis. It's also possible, as Rutgers University psychologist David Brodzinsky has found, that the hurt caused by having once been relinquished causes adoptees to "remain vulnerable."

And it's possible—I think it's quite likely—that there are genetic factors that place many children at risk. The fact is, while we are able to know a good deal about the birth mother and her family history, in far too many instances our knowledge of the genetic background of the birth father and his family is either scanty or nonexistent. *Adoptive parents have to be people who are willing to trust, to take some risks, and to accept challenges. If you cannot take some risks, adoption is not for you.*

Now let's focus on the up side. Studies of adoption outcomes have also affirmed that *most* adoptees do very well in life. How, then, do we explain the negative perception of adoption that is furthered by this myth? It seems to me that every time something bad happens and an adoptee is involved, it makes the headlines. But when a biological child runs away from home, or gets into trouble, or causes harm to his or her parents, people don't comment, "Of course, what can you expect from a youngster who was born into his family!"

I think that adopted kids often get a raw deal when the media insist on describing them as "adopted children" forever. (I really dislike this label, which too often is permanently affixed to people who have been adopted, like the mattress tags that warn, "Do not remove under penalty of law.") We do have to be aware of labels and the connotations that people often attach to them.

I have seen families look on with pride as their adopted child had a walk-on role in the first-grade play or skated to a gold medal in the Olympics. I have seen parents badly shaken when their biological child flunks out of school or runs into some trouble with the law. As a result of my experiences in dealing with families (and they're fairly extensive by now), I am convinced that raising children is likely to include both delights and disappointments—without regard to how the children initially became members of the family.

6

The Truth About Birth Mothers

Suppose, now, that you're no longer simply "thinking" about adopting, that by this time both you and your spouse are seriously considering adoption as the best possible means of building your family. Perhaps you've already taken one or more of the following steps toward making this happen: placed phone calls to various social service agencies and independent adoption facilitators; explored intercountry adoption; attended introductory meetings at a couple of agencies to learn about their policies and practices; maybe you've even gone so far as to fill out an application form or two. At any rate, you've reached a place in life where you find adoption changing from a pipe dream to a possible reality for you.

Up to this point, there's been but one focus of that dream: a baby. Right about here, however, you may be finding that the dream's beginning to get just a little bit crowded. Other characters (social workers, doctors, lawyers) have started nudging their way in. You're beginning to hear a lot about the birth parents—especially the birth mother. More than likely, some of the talk causes you to toss and turn.

While I hope that this chapter will go far in addressing your uneasiness, I'd also like to assure you that experiencing some discomfort with this subject is both natural and understandable. Introducing the concept of birth parents forces you to come face to face with a truth that you might have preferred to gloss over: the child who becomes your son or daughter through adoption will also have another set of parents—the people responsible for his or her existence.

Acknowledging the birth parents can lead to other thoughts, among them: *What kind of people are they? What does their medical and psychological history look like? What are the circumstances that led them to decide against raising the child themselves? Are they apt to change their minds and attempt to disrupt the adoption?* In the dreams of those who begin to pursue adoption, the birth parent often appears as a kind of bogeyman (a bogeywoman, to be more accurate). It is a nightmare that must be addressed and replaced by reality. I promise you that it can, and will, go away as you learn more about the birth parents *and* as you begin to create a lifelong bond with your child.

My own story serves as an example. When Weezie and I adopted Josh, we were just as paranoid as the next couple. I'd be less than honest if I didn't admit that I was even somewhat relieved when we weren't given any identifying information about his birth parents, nor they about us. Circumstances change. It's now one of the regrets of my life that we didn't meet, and that I cannot share with Josh's other parents the special joy that comes with knowing our son.

This chapter will help you learn more about birth parents in general by shedding some light on who they are, some of their reasons for deciding to plan adoption for their babies, and what *they* look for in an adoptive couple. I believe that the more you know, the less anxious you will be when the subject of birth parents is raised—both now when you're hoping to adopt, and later when your child comes to you and asks questions.

It may help to look at it this way. Adoption is a process. The way you think and feel about the birth parents of your child is evolutionary. It is part of that process.

ADDRESSING THE STEREOTYPES

In our meetings with adoptive applicants at Golden Cradle, we begin the learning process by encouraging participants in our groups to give voice to the stereotypical images that they or others may hold about the kind of person who would create a child and then place the child for adoption.

Imagining the Birth Mother

What kind of person is she? When adoptive applicants envision the child's other parents, the birth mother is the one they typically focus on. They wonder: What is she like and how did she happen to get herself pregnant? Often, the public perception of a person who gives her child up for adoption is of some sleazy woman who stands on the street corner and sleeps around. That couldn't be further from the mark. In the first place, women who have sex for a living know how to prevent pregnancy. They have to . . . or they're out of work. And if they do have an "accident," many choose to have an abortion.

Here's another way the birth mother is often pictured. "When I was in high school," recalled a woman in one of our groups, "there was this girl in our class who got into trouble. She was known to be fast. In fact, you didn't want to be seen with her because then *you'd* get a reputation. To no one's surprise, one day we heard that she was pregnant and by the next day she had been whisked away. When I think about birth mothers, *she's* what I think they are like."

Is this pretty much the way that you envision someone who becomes pregnant and chooses adoption for her baby? Do you have different images?

I'd like to take you through an exercise that we do with the husbands and wives with whom we work at Golden Cradle. Imagine, then, that you are sitting around a conference table with several other couples who, like you, are in the process of exploring adoption as a viable way of building their family. Picture a social worker guiding your discussion. She stands before a blackboard at the front of the room. Chalk in hand, she writes across the board in large white letters: *Birth mother*.

"We're going to make a list of adjectives that people might use in describing birth mothers," she says. "What are the images that are out there? Don't be embarrassed to say whatever comes to your mind. What shall I put down in this column?"

"She's probably a teenager," someone offers. Underneath the heading, the social worker scrawls *Teenager*.

"She isn't married," suggests another of the people seated at the table. *Unwed*, the social worker writes.

Slowly and steadily the list grows longer as people call out: "She's fast" . . . "someone from the wrong side of the tracks" . . . "irresponsible" . . . "vulnerable" . . . "poor" . . . "uneducated" . . . "young" . . . "religious" . . . "into drugs" . . . "a substance abuser" . . . "naive" . . . "a victim."

Among these responses, are there any that you might have offered? Are some of these characteristics the ones that come to *your* mind when you think about what a birth mother might be like?

Imagining the Birth Father

The social worker creates a second column, labeling it *Birth father*. A collective groan goes up from the group even before she gets to ask the question that everyone has already anticipated: "What words should I put down to describe how the birth father is perceived?"

The list that emerges in response to this question is longer. It's clear that, when it comes to the birth fathers, members of the group feel no compunction to hold back. "He's an s.o.b.," one of the husbands calls out, as everyone laughs. "A deceiver," offers someone else in the room. The descriptions that follow are largely derogatory: "liar" . . . "heartless" . . . "Joe Jock" . . . "macho" . . . "college student" . . . "absent" . . . "substance abuser" . . . "married" . . . "irresponsible" . . . "stud" . . . "unknown."

Did you hear *your* voice here? If you think about the birth father at all (and most adopting parents tend to assign him a minor role, if any, in their fantasies), do these descriptions fit the stereotypes you hold?

COUNTERING THE STEREOTYPES

Introducing the Birth Mothers

The most effective way that I know of to destroy a stereotype is to have people come in contact with the real thing. That's what worked for me. In the first three and a half years of operating Golden Cradle, I interviewed 440 birth mothers. They ranged in age from thirteen to forty-two. Some were children. Some were college students. Some were married, many of them raising children who were born to them previously. The child they placed for adoption was the one who, due to both timing and circumstances, the family simply could not accommodate. Others were married but pregnant by men who were not their spouses. The fact is, more than 25 percent of the people who come to us for help in placing their children for adoption are married couples.

If I had to describe the average birth mother seen at Golden Cradle, though, I'd place her between eighteen and twenty-two years of age. She's either in school or working. She isn't married. For six out of ten women, this is their first pregnancy. Although some similarities do emerge (as would be likely in a sizable sample of any given group), I'd still have to conclude that birth mothers on the whole do not fit any formula.

The Turnaround Meeting

Having invited you to sit in on the meeting at which birth-parent stereotypes were raised, I now ask you to imagine yourself attending the "turnaround meeting" where they're demolished. Today's agenda includes hearing from a panel of birth mothers who chose to place their children for adoption. Husbands and wives who go through our program tend to speak of this one meeting as *the* pivotal event that helped destroy and lay to rest the birth-parent stereotypes that had been making them feel uneasy. One man in the audience later describes the impact on him this way: "Suddenly the faceless stranger has a face."

You're about to see what that face looks like.

The room is crowded. Once people have settled down, the moderator opens the day's program by introducing three attractive young women who are seated at the front, facing the audience. The women have all placed their babies with adoptive families. How and why they reached this decision is the substance of the stories they go on to tell. Let's listen.

Marylou's Story

Marylou rises and walks up to the microphone. She's of medium height. Her light brown hair stops just short of her shoulders, framing an oval face with deep-set brown eyes. She's a pretty woman who looks half a dozen years younger than her thirty-four years. Marylou tells the audience that she attended college for two years and now holds down a good job with an insurance company. She also informs us that she was married to the father when her baby was conceived.

"The marriage was a disaster," she says ruefully. "In fact, my whole romance with Jeff was a disaster. He could be very charming, but he had a volatile temper when he drank too much . . . and he drank too much too often. I met Jeff at a dinner party arranged by mutual friends. We quickly discovered that we both liked to travel, and we spent a lot of time talking about places we'd been to and destinations we hoped to visit. Jeff had done a lot of backpacking through the Far East, for example, and I found his stories fascinating.

"We dated for about ten months, during which time we kept breaking up and getting back together. Jeff would get very possessive and then, when things seemed good between us, he'd suddenly grow distant. I think that his mood swings were connected to a turbulent childhood, and at one point (I'm not sure why) I decided that marriage might be the answer. Maybe Jeff would feel more secure. Maybe I could change him. So we married, and our relationship went quickly from bad to worse.

I was seriously considering walking out of the marriage when, two months after the wedding, I found out I was pregnant. It was bad news that couldn't have come at a worse time.

"For a brief while things began to calm down," Marylou continues. "The pregnancy gave Jeff and me a reason to try to work things out. But the responsibility of a coming baby proved to be too much for Jeff, who seemed always ready to hit the road again. He became very angry, and started blaming me for getting us into this predicament. He wanted me to have an abortion, which is just something that I do not believe in. When I told him that I planned to have the baby, Jeff grew physically and emotionally abusive. I was in my sixth month when we separated. I knew then that I had some very important decisions to make. One thing was clear to me: I could not raise a baby by myself.

"The bottom line for me was that I did not want to have a permanent connection to this man, and I knew that a child would serve to bind us together for life, no matter whether we stayed married or not. I also wanted something better for the child than what I'd be able to provide if I had to stay at home as a single mother. I had read a story about Golden Cradle in a popular magazine, and I decided to find out what the agency was about. When I called and came in, I learned that I could have a say in what *I* wanted for the baby. I won't tell you that the ability to be involved made placing my daughter easy, but I will tell you that it made the decision easier to live with because I *know* she is with a good family. I chose them myself."

Marylou asked to select and meet with the adoptive parents before her baby was born. (Jeff refused to be involved in anything having to do with the baby except for signing the surrender of parental rights after the little girl was born.) Because her marriage had been troubled from the start, Marylou felt that she needed to get some feeling for the strength of the adoptive couple's commitment to one another—to be assured that they would be there, together, to raise the child. She also wanted to learn from the couple about how they handled disagreements. "I would not have placed my daughter in an environment where people shouted at one another or were in any other way abusive," Marylou says. "It matters very much to me that she is being brought up in a home where there is mutual respect between her father and mother.

"That was two years ago," Marylou continues. "Since then, the adoptive parents have been sending me reports of her progress, including photographs, fairly regularly—once a month for the first six months and then about every half year or so. We've spoken by phone too. When my divorce became final, I sent them a note through the agency, and they called me. I also wanted them to know that things were going well for me at work. I think that knowing that I'm in a good place helps them feel more comfortable . . . and I do believe they want the best for me. As for *my* wants, I need to know that our daughter is fine. That's the way I think about the situation: that they are the parents, but she is 'our daughter.' I am thankful that they are giving her a good life."

Janine's Story

Eighteen-year-old Janine is introduced next. The audience sees a large-boned young woman who stands about five feet six inches in sneakers, wears her blonde hair full and curly, has wide green eyes accented by green eye shadow, and is dressed in jeans and a bulky knit sweater with a teddy bear design running across the front. Less than six months have elapsed since Janine gave birth to a baby boy, whom she placed for adoption. When we asked Janine if she wished to be part of the birth-mother panel, she was quick to agree. "It's important for people to know that this kind of thing goes on," she told her caseworker. What kind of thing? "I was a victim of date rape," she tells the people in the audience. "That's how I became pregnant."

In her talk, Janine never identifies her assailant by name. It's as if she doesn't want to give him the dignity of an introduction. "I met the father of my baby one Saturday when I went to the mall with some friends," she declares. "I was seventeen, and had just entered my junior year of high school. He was twenty-one and worked in one of the fast-food restaurants in the mall. I thought he was cute and I suppose I flirted with him, thinking maybe he would ask me out. A few weeks later, when I went back to the mall and stopped by to talk to him again, he did.

"He wasn't my first boyfriend," Janine continues, "but I wasn't very experienced either. We went out a couple of times, mostly to the movies and afterward we'd park and kind of neck and wrestle until I'd say no and let him know that we'd gone far enough. I can't say that I led him on (I've thought about that a lot since then) because I made it clear from the start that I wasn't about to go all the way.

"This one time he asked me to go back with him to his apartment. We could listen to some albums, he said. I had never before dated anyone who had his own place, and I wasn't sure that I ought to go. But he said we'd only stop by for about an hour, and then he'd take me home. So I went.

"At his house—actually, it was a room that he rented in somebody's basement—we both had a beer and then things began to get out of hand," Janine continues. "I told him I wanted to go home, but he wouldn't let me leave. I said I meant it—I wanted to go right then and there. He grabbed me and forced himself on me. I couldn't believe what was happening. I didn't have the strength to make him stop. I didn't tell anyone about what happened—not my parents, not even my closest friend. I felt so dirty. I stopped going to the mall so that I wouldn't run into him. I never wanted to see or hear from him again."

Janine skipped her period, but ignored it. The first month, then the second, then the third went by. "I kept telling myself, 'You *can't* get pregnant the first time you do it,' and I really believed that. I didn't think it could happen. As you'll soon see, I denied a lot. One day my mom walked into my room. She looked at me and said, 'You're gaining a lot of weight. Are you pregnant?' I told her it wasn't possible, but she still insisted on taking me to see a doctor. The very next day we found out that I was in my eighth month. My mom was the one who phoned Golden Cradle."

(Typically, the birth parents we see do not rush off to the gynecologist the first time they miss having a period. They wait to seek medical attention until some time in their second trimester, but Janine had waited longer than most. The concern of the staff at Golden Cradle, therefore, was to see to Janine's medical care even before we addressed her emotional needs. She not only had to recognize the pregnancy, she needed to decide—pretty quickly—what she was going do about it. Janine's parents are divorced, and she does not see her father, but her mother was very much involved in the decision. She was not only concerned about her daughter, but she also cared about the welfare of her soon-to-be-born first grandchild! It was not an easy time for this family. It never is.)

"My mom and I talked the situation over. My uncle wanted to go to the police and have them arrest the guy, but I begged him not to. I didn't want to have to answer any questions or to be forced to see him again. (I *haven't* seen him since the baby was born, but the agency did call him and tell him about the baby.) The way I looked at it, nothing that any of us could do would make the pregnancy go away. So the thing that my mom and I needed to talk about was what we were going to do about the baby.

"The main issue for me was that the baby not suffer because of something that was not its fault," Janine explains. "If anything good could come out of this, my mom and I decided, it would be that the baby would go on to have a good life. I wanted him to be able to grow up with a mother and father who both wanted him and who would both take care of him. I wanted a family that would be active and do things together, not just sit around and watch television. And I wanted a family that would be real excited when they found out they were going to become parents. So that's the family I chose, and they really seem to be good people. They have sent me pictures twice so far. The baby is smiling now. He looks like our family . . . especially around the eyes."

Lisa's Story

Lisa, twenty, is a pretty girl with reddish brown hair that she wears in a braid down her back. She has deep brown eyes that gaze directly at the audience. Lisa attends a state university, she tells the couples who have gathered for this meeting, where she is in her junior year. She *had* been planning earlier on spending her junior year abroad, she adds, but she hadn't counted on becoming pregnant last year. Lisa is a planner, which is why she still finds it hard to believe that her planning—including the cautious use of birth control—could have gone so awry.

"I met Zach, who's the baby's father, during freshman orientation week at college," Lisa says. "He was one of the sophomore advisers assigned to our group. I know that this sounds like a line from a grade-B movie, but it's true: the moment I saw Zach I knew he was the man for me."

She goes on: "He didn't seem quite so smitten—although he tells me now that he was attracted to me right away too. If that's true, he did a pretty good job of keeping it a secret. We would run into one another on campus from time to time, and sometimes we'd stop and talk. That was about the extent of our relationship until I phoned Zach, one evening, and invited him to be my date for the Halloween Ball being given by my sorority. He accepted . . . and we've been together ever since."

As Lisa describes it, she and Zach soon were "in a relationship," which means that they dated each other exclusively. "We were very careful," says Lisa. "We both were concerned about the long-term effects of birth control pills, so I used a diaphragm—and found out that it wasn't foolproof.

"When I told Zach that I was pregnant, he said we should get married right away. I mean, there was no question in both our minds that someday we *would* marry, but we also had decided that we didn't want to rush into it. Our plan was to finish school—including graduate school—and get started on our careers before settling down and raising a family. Another thing that is important to me is that I didn't want Zach to marry me *because* of the baby. When the time is right, I want to feel that we're marrying because we want to, not because we have to. I don't believe in abortion, and so we decided to have the baby and then to place it with a couple who could give our child *now* what we hope we'll be able to provide for a child maybe ten years from now."

Lisa and Zach came to the agency when Lisa was in her third month of pregnancy. To spare her family discomfort, Lisa took a semester off from school and entered Golden Cradle's housing program. She lived with one of our families and found work through a temporary employment agency. She and Zach also insisted on selecting and meeting the couple who would adopt their child—they had a girl—several months before the birth. They asked the adoptive parents if they wished to be in the delivery room when the baby was born. (They did, and count themselves privileged to have shared the experience with the birth parents. The two couples continue to be in contact.)

"The way we feel about our daughter's adoptive parents," Lisa stresses, "is that *they* are her parents. There's no question in our minds about that. We are grateful to them for doing something we would not have been able to do at this time—giving our baby a wonderful life. We are also grateful because they haven't shut us out of that life."

So now you've met three birth mothers. I am not going to tell you that all birth mothers are innocent young girls (although many are) or that the majority are women who have been taken advantage of. The fact is that some birth mothers *are* promiscuous, and some are careless, and some are too drug and alcohol dependent to give thought to the consequences of the sexual activity in which they engage. But I am going to tell you that the vast majority, in my experience, are greatly concerned about the welfare of their children.

One of our adoptive applicants said it very well when he told me, "Before I attended this meeting, I pictured the birth mother as not a caring person. The stigma attached to 'giving away a baby' was there in my thoughts of her. Now I understand that the norm is the exact opposite, and that 'giving a baby away' is not selfish, but a decision reached *because* she is caring. She wants more for her baby than she herself can provide."

He added, "Having met the birth mothers, I am also far less concerned about their coming to get the baby someday. The more information you get about something you fear, the less you will fear it." I couldn't have put it better myself!

Introducing the Birth Fathers

I find it easier to talk about birth mothers than I do about birth fathers. For one thing, while we *always* know who the mother of the child is, in far too many situations the birth father's identity is either questionable or unknown. For another, I haven't had many good experiences with birth fathers. In the more than four hundred interviews with birth parents that I conducted, there were at most twenty-five times when the birth mothers and birth fathers came in together. When I did manage to contact the men who were involved, I was likely to hear: "How do you know it was me?" or "I wasn't the only one."

Marlene Piasecki, executive director of Golden Cradle, is responsible for the current workings of the agency, however, and she tells me that the situation is different now. More birth fathers are involved. In large part, that positive development is a long-term result of *Stanley v. Illinois,* a 1972 decision in which the U.S. Supreme Court held that the rights of unwed birth fathers could not be terminated without due process of law.

The courts in most states now require that every legal effort be made to find the birth father and inform him of the pregnancy. In practical terms, this also means that any responsible agency, like Golden Cradle, will do its level best to identify and locate the birth father and involve him in planning for the baby. If the birth father can't be located or if he *is* found and is unwilling either to raise the child or to execute a consent (or surrender) of parental rights, then those rights must be legally terminated by the courts.

We do run into situations in which the birth mother is unwilling to name the father of the child she is carrying. When we tell her that we are legally required to search for him, we will often hear, "But if I go privately, the lawyer says that I don't have to name the birth father." (That just isn't so.) If you decide to adopt independently and you're told that the birth father is "unknown," I urge you to find out what efforts have been made to establish his identity and inform him of the child's existence. It's better to be careful now than regretful later.

"In at least one-quarter of our cases, the birth father truly cannot be located," says Marlene Piasecki. "In another quarter, we find him but he's unwilling to acknowledge paternity. Then there's a third quarter in which the birth fathers approve of the adoption plan and will sign the necessary papers. But in the final twenty-five percent of cases, the birth fathers are right there—supporting the birth mothers, taking preparation-for-birth classes along with the women, anguishing over the placement decision, and grieving the loss of the child they will not get to raise. Of this group, some will decide to raise the child themselves."

I cannot recreate a panel of birth fathers for you here (we have not yet set up such a panel to address our applicants at Golden Cradle), but I have tried to do the next best thing by asking members of our staff to describe several birth fathers with whom they have worked. As the stories of the birth fathers emerge, it is clear that they are real players in the drama of adoption. And many of them really do care.

Meet David

David had yet to celebrate his seventeenth birthday when he became a father. He had been seeing Nicole, a pretty blond cheerleader in his class, for about six months when her parents went off on a week's vacation, leaving their daughter at home alone. The young couple saw this as an opportunity for sexual experimentation. "That's all it was," David says. "I thought if you withdrew, you'd never make a girl pregnant." The dark-eyed teenager shakes his head in disbelief. "We sure found out otherwise."

When Nicole suspected that she was pregnant, David went with her to the clinic. They learned the news together, then went back to their respective homes to tell their parents. "My mother cried," says David. "My father phoned Nicole's parents and we set up a meeting to decide what to do. When I arrived at Nicole's home, her father glared at me as if I were scum. That's the kind of treatment I got throughout Nicole's pregnancy. Everybody rallied around her, and everybody treated me like I was some kind of heartless stud. Heck, the idea of our having sex was as much Nicole's as mine. I mean, she's been my first and only sexual partner too."

There was no question of the couple's marrying. They were much too young. Nicole's parents wanted her to keep the baby, whom they would help raise, and David agreed to take a job after school and contribute to the baby's support if that became the plan. But Nicole hoped to go away to college someday, and did not see how she could do that and leave the baby in her parents' care. She felt that they would then be the parents, not she and David. Reluctantly, the young couple decided to place the child for adoption.

"Nicole and I still go out," says David, "but we won't even kiss. We're *that* afraid of the consequences."

Meet Tony

Tony's education stopped in the tenth grade. Now twenty-one, he works for a landscaping company. It's seasonal work, good when you can get it. While Tony enjoys what he does, he wishes he could find something steadier. Tony met Alice, who is sixteen, in the neighborhood and they had a couple of dates, nothing serious. As is true for so many young people, sex was a regular part of an evening out for them. Contraception was not, and so Alice became pregnant.

She has not yet had the child, but Alice and her parents have told their caseworker that there is absolutely no possibility of her raising a baby. Alice is too young, they explained. She also has a younger brother and sister at home who must be considered. As soon as they learned of the pregnancy, Alice's parents decided on having the baby adopted. Their daughter went along with the decision.

The agency contacted Tony.

His caseworker reports, "The young man who came in to meet me is a very decent fellow, hard-working and responsible. He is not in love with Alice and, especially because she is so young, he does not plan to marry her. Tony was not happy to learn about the coming baby but he is also in conflict about placing the child for adoption. On the one hand, he knows that he cannot ask a sixteen-year-old to become a single mom. On the other hand, he is finding it very hard to surrender his parental rights. He feels that he is working and ought to be able to support a child."

The first thing the counselor did was convince Tony that it was important for him to tell his parents. She knew that he would need support from his family as he grappled with his decision. She tells what happened next: "After Tony's mother came off the ceiling and calmed down, she told him that she would help him as best she could. Because she has a job, Tony's mother could not promise to stay at home and care for the baby—he would have to make child-care arrangements for when he was at work—but she would make room in her home for her grandchild and generally try to be of some assistance, she told him.

"Tony also talked with Alice's parents and is aware that they are pressuring their daughter to place the child," his worker continues. "They've told him in no uncertain terms that they will not share the caretaking or financial responsibilities and that his procrastination is making life difficult for them. But Tony feels that he cannot just say yes in order to make everyone happy. As the delivery date draws closer, we continue to be there for him—to help him sort out his wishes, his pains, and his concerns."

Meet Patrick

Patrick, thirty-two, is married and has a son and daughter. It's not a very happy marriage, but neither is it a relationship he intends to walk away from. "Family" is a value that Patrick was raised to respect. A little dalliance on the side (there'd been several brief diversions over the years) didn't in any way affect that basic commitment.

Patrick is a policeman. To earn extra money, he works evenings at a local movie house. That's where he met Terri, an eighteen-year-old college student. From the start, Patrick told her that he was married. He even proudly showed her pictures of his children. Terri didn't intend to get involved either. She liked to kid around with Patrick, liked having him phone her at the dormitory and come by to take her out for an hour or two. It was not an affair; it was a flirtation—one that simply went too far.

When Terri came to Golden Cradle, she had her mind made up. She planned to have the baby, to continue with school (fortunately, the due date fell between semesters), and to have us work with her toward an adoption.

And where was Patrick, the birth father, in all this? "He was there to acknowledge paternity," says his counselor, "and to support Terri's placement decision. For Patrick, parenting this child was never a possibility. He didn't want anybody— especially his wife—to find out what had happened. That was so important to him that the only way the agency could get in touch with him was to write to a post office box which he rented expressly for that purpose. Still, Patrick was a full participant with Terri in planning for the baby's permanent placement. It was important to him that the adoptive parents be 'regular folks, people who would have lots of time to spend with the kid.' He also was insistent that the baby be placed with a family where the mother would stay at home full time . . . like his wife."

WHAT BIRTH PARENTS WANT TO KNOW

Another way to gain a better understanding of what birth parents are all about is to listen to the concerns they express as they deal with the problems raised by an unintended pregnancy and as they struggle to resolve what is good for them and what is best for the child. I have always felt that it is a privilege to be able to help in that process. It is also a tremendous responsibility.

When birth mothers or their families reach us, one of the first things they want to ascertain is that we are a licensed, legitimate agency. (That's something that many adoptive parents want to know too.)

They also want to make sure that they will not be signing away their parental rights if they decide to enter our program, that they will have both time and opportunity to consider their options. We can easily give them these assurances. Whenever we work with birth parents, we help them develop several strategies—not just an adoption plan. I feel strongly that every agency, attorney, religious leader . . . anyone consulted by a birth parent in this situation should do no less.

Furthermore, it is *illegal* to have the birth parent sign a "consent to adopt" (also known as a surrender) before the baby is born. There are good reasons for this law, mostly having to do with respecting the birth mother's requirement for time to adjust to the fact that she's just had a baby and her need to resolve the feelings brought on by the event. This applies to birth fathers as well.

Experience has taught me that anything can happen during this waiting period—and it sometimes does. It is not unusual for a birth mother who planned adoption all during her pregnancy to change her mind when an actual baby is nestled in her arms and decide that, one way or another, she is going to raise this baby herself. I've also seen young women who intended to keep their babies change *their* plans after the baby is born. They realize that the infant is not a toy and requires more care than they can provide at this time. Suddenly, adoption becomes the plan.

It is important, therefore, to allow the birth parents some time postpartum to reconsider their feelings and reflect on their choices. The actual length of time that must elapse between the baby's birth and signing of the consent, however, differs from state to state, as do the procedures involved. For example, in our home state of New Jersey, a signed surrender may be taken from the birth parents no sooner than seventy-two hours following the child's birth. Pennsylvania (which also mandates a minimum waiting time of seventy-two hours) additionally requires that the consent be confirmed by the court, generally forty to fifty days later.

The birth parents who contact us are concerned about their medical care. They ask about the doctors we refer patients to, the hospitals where they will give birth if they choose to deliver locally. Some ask whether they will be able to continue to see their own obstetricians. Yes, we tell them, they can use their own obstetricians or the ones we recommend. We stress the importance of good prenatal care.

Many birth mothers are interested in learning whether housing is available (yes); sometimes, they ask about whether we offer a living allowance. (Some ask us to pay their rent because, they explain, they have had to quit their jobs. One birth mother asked for thirty-five thousand dollars to maintain her style of living. In all of these situations, our answer must be, "No, that is illegal." The birth mothers go elsewhere.)

Birth parents also ask us:

— Where do the adoptive couples come from? [Most of our clients live in the Philadelphia, New Jersey, Delaware region.]
— How do you choose them? What is the home study process like? [We explain our criteria for adoption.]
— How soon after birth is the baby placed? [Most birth parents do not want the child to go into foster care. They would like the infant to be placed with his or her permanent family as soon as possible. We do our best to make this happen although we are finding that many hospitals now release mothers and babies as early as twenty-four or forty-eight hours following a trouble-free delivery and healthy birth. Because the consent cannot be signed until seventy-two hours have elapsed, the baby may need to be placed very briefly in foster care. Sometimes the adoptive couple is willing to take the risk of accepting the infant (as short-term foster parents) even though a surrender has not yet been signed. At other times, the baby may have to be placed with an approved foster family before moving to its permanent home.

Today, more and more birth parents are asking for some sort of openness in the adoption. (See chapter 9.) They want to make certain that they will have as much information as they need or want about the adopting couple. Many ask:

— Can I be involved in selecting the couple? [Yes.]
— Can I talk to them? [Yes.]
— Will it be possible for me to meet them? [Yes. We will see to it that the baby is matched with adoptive parents who are comfortable in accepting this condition.]

Many of the questions reflect the birth parents' concern about the baby's future. They ask:

— If the infant is born with a disabling condition or other problem, will you still place the baby with a permanent family? [Yes, but it may not be with the couple originally chosen. Still, the birth parent can expect to take part in the placement decision.]
— What happens if the adoptive couple decides to divorce after the adoption has been finalized? [Custody and support decisions would be made as in any other family where divorce takes place.]

What Birth Parents Hope to Find in an Adoptive Couple

Most of the birth parents I have known want a loving, secure, stable family that will be able to manage what they can not do at the time: successfully raise a child. Some ask the agency to select that family for them. The vast majority, however, are more comfortable knowing that they have the option to be involved in selecting the family. But the qualities that they look for in the families they choose are as different and diverse as the people who are doing the choosing. Consider the following:

— Some birth parents want their baby to go to a family that already has other children. "I enjoyed growing up in a large family," they say, "and I want my child to have a similar experience."

- Other birth parents specifically request that the baby go to a childless husband and wife, preferably "to a couple that's been waiting a long time."
- Certain of our birth parents express a religious preference. They would like the child to be raised in an environment that is familiar to them.
- Many birth parents inquire into the couple's feelings about discipline. It matters a great deal to them that no corporal punishment will be used in raising the child.
- They also want to make sure that there's no alcoholism or drug abuse problem in the adopting household. (Again, what they're looking for is a stable family.)
- Quite a few of our birth parents request an adoptive family with a stay-at-home parent (or one in which the couple has flexible work schedules so they can arrange to spend a lot of time with the child).
- Still others prefer a professional couple, one that will be able to offer the child all the advantages.
- Some birth parents ask about the education of the adoptive parents. They're eager to place with a family that will encourage the child to go on to college and, when the time arrives, make it possible for him or her to do so.
- Others prefer families like the ones in which they grew up, or the ones they hope to be part of in their own marriages someday.
- Some of our birth parents are attracted to younger couples, and some prefer older, more mature parents.

I could go on. For example: Some birth parents express a preference for couples who are active in sports; others are drawn to people involved in volunteer activities. Sometimes hobbies set one couple apart from another; in other situations, the fact that the family has a pet may be seen as an asset. (This is not a signal, however, to rush right out and buy a dog or cat in order to enhance your profile.)

I have gone into the question of "what birth parents look for in adoptive parents" at some length because I know that, in this age of increasing openness in adoption, it can create a good deal of anxiety in couples who spend a lot of time wondering, *Will we be chosen?*

Rest assured, you will. My advice to you on this score is to just be yourself. One of the myths surrounding the selection process is that when birth parents are involved in selecting the adoptive parents, the couple they choose will be the one with the most education, biggest home, and best looks. To believe that their decision is no more than a beauty contest is to underestimate the birth parents' concern for the child and the gravity with which they make this decision.

7

What Adoptive Applicants Look Like and What They Want to Know

Marie, thirty-six, recalls:

> It was the evening of the introductory gathering at the adoption agency. Ken and I were nervous as we entered the meeting room and eyed the other men and women, about twenty-five couples in all. Like us, we knew they were here because they had decided it was time to pursue adoption and they hoped that the agency would agree to work with them. Like us, too, they looked ill at ease. *Which of us would make it?*
>
> Folding chairs had been set up for this meeting. The two front rows were empty. We sought out seats in the rear, which seemed to be going at a premium. As I looked about me, I tried to assess our chances. Did Ken and I look too old to adopt? Too young? Did the other couples smile at each other more often? Did they seem more compatible than we were? Did they appear more successful? I wondered what they did for a living. I wondered how long they had been married and how long they had been trying to have a baby. Had we reached this stage too soon? Had we waited too long?
>
> Later, when some members of the group spoke up, I remember thinking: did the questions they asked show them to be more thoughtful, more knowledgeable about adoption? How did the agency *feel* about people asking questions? Should Ken or I raise our hands during the question-and-answer session, showing interest, or would it be better to keep a low profile and strive to remain anonymous? There

was no place for spontaneity here. Caution was the name of the game.

Three and a half years have gone by since that day. Ken and Marie are now parents, by adoption, to eleven-month-old Michelle. For the most part, they are much more confident about themselves as individuals, as husband and wife, and as parents. But every once in a while the feelings of self-doubt and the panic of self-assessment briefly reappear. A part of them may always wonder: are we worthy of this child?

As I began to plan this chapter, the thought occurred to me: *What am I doing, introducing my reader to couples who are seeking to adopt?* If *you* are a prospective adoptive parent, you don't have to be told what people who are interested in adopting a baby look and think like. You understand their concerns and you know their aspirations. You know all of this because the adoptive applicant is you.

How You Look in Stereotype: Imagining the Adoptive Parents

You may be surprised, however, to learn a few things about how you are perceived by others. Just as many couples come to adoption carrying time-worn images of what birth parents are like, many birth parents begin the adoption process with skewed notions about the kinds of people who become parents by adoption.

If the birth parents were challenged to create a list of these stereotypes (in much the same manner that the adoptive applicants in the previous chapter were asked to), I have no doubt (from talking with birth parents) that the following descriptions might appear: yuppies; possessive; paranoid—forever scared that the birth mother will come back to reclaim her child; sad; rich people "buying" kids; privileged; older; workaholics; frigid. The list would also include the following attributes: good people; loving; generous; kind.

When we instituted our housing program at Golden Cradle, we didn't anticipate that one of the major benefits to result from having birth parents live with couples waiting to adopt was that, in coming together, each would shed the stereotypical images they had of the other. Here's how one of our birth mothers describes the experience: "When I agreed to go into housing with Paula and Fred, who were in the process of adopting, I have to admit that I felt a lot of resentment toward them. Without even knowing them, I felt that they represented everything I wanted but could not have: a marriage; a regular income; a house; and, most of all, the ability to care for a child. The way I looked at it, they were the haves and I was the have-not."

She continues, "Until I lived with them, I had never thought about the terrible struggle that some people go through to have a baby and how it feels when you find out that it's not going to happen. Sure they had a house, but the nursery was empty. Paula had a great job, but she would have given up her career in a minute for the chance to become a mother. It wasn't at all like they were buying a baby; it was more that they were doing everything possible in order to be able to have a child in their lives. When I heard later that they adopted a little boy, I really was happy because I knew how much it meant to them."

Different Couples, Different Stories

It also seems to me that, while you're familiar with your own story (the reasons you're now considering adoption), you just might be interested in learning about the variety of backgrounds and experiences that others bring to becoming adoptive parents. I am not talking here about such things as age, ethnicity, the communities that people live in, or the ways in which they earn their living. Adoptive parents come from many walks of life and their personal stories reflect that diversity. As would be expected, there also are many striking commonalities. For instance: Just say the words *Clomid* or *laparoscopy* in any gathering of people who are applying to adopt. Try *sperm count*. Mention that your mother-in-law has been asking when you're finally going to get around to giving her a grandchild. A general groan will rise up from the group. Everybody, it seems, has been there. Everyone in the room understands.

Still, within the group there are stories that you might *not* expect to find, accounts that offer a unique perspective on the adoption experience. Who are the adopters? Let me introduce you to two adoptive mothers who generously gave permission to share their stories, asking only that their names be changed in this retelling.

Meet Robin

The adoptive-parent population includes many people who were themselves adopted. Robin is in this group. At thirty-eight, Robin looks like the women featured in Ralph Lauren ads—women with a kind of natural beauty that stands out against a rural background. Women who seem comfortable with themselves and their surroundings. "I am the adoptive parent of a two-year-old son," says Robin, describing her situation. "I am also an adopted child." Therein lies her story.

"Taken home" by her adoptive parents when she was three days old, Robin grew up as a much-loved child who always knew she was adopted and could turn to her parents when questions arose. "My questions were answered as honestly as possible," she says, "but I also felt that I didn't have a right to ask about certain things. For instance, I felt uncomfortable pressing my parents for details about my birth mother. I saw it as a loyalty issue, and I didn't want to cause any hurt."

She continues, "I grew up feeling, as a lot of adoptees do, that I wasn't born, that I just happened. I longed to see somebody whom I looked like. My adoptive mother was a tiny lady who never weighed much more than ninety pounds. By the age of twelve, I was bigger than she, and I felt so gawky. Having a photograph of my birth mother would have been very helpful at that time. It could have offered me some hope for the woman I would become.

"I especially looked forward to marrying and having children so I could have a genetic link to *someone*," Robin says. "When I did marry and my husband and I found out that the only way we could make a family was through adoption, I felt cheated. But I soon got over that and began looking forward to adopting a child.

"I wanted to do things differently in raising this child than had been done with me. I wanted to give the child a strong sense that he was born, not just raised. So I started keeping a journal of the adoption, of our feelings from the time we received the agency acceptance letter . . . to our son Ben's arrival . . . to the 'sharing sheets' about Ben's progress that we sent, each month, to his birth mother. Gradually, I began to understand that in documenting Ben's present life I was also trying to reconstruct my past. I realized that the way I could be most effective for him was to search for my birth family."

All accounts of search and reunion are dramatic and Robin's was no exception. Robin's adoptive mother had died, but her father was able to provide the names of her birth mother and the hospital where Robin was born. Armed with this information and helped by members of a local adoptees support group, Robin located her birth mother. She says, "Making the phone call that might open up a whole new dimension to my life was the more difficult task. It required a lot of courage. It took me a long time to do it."

The reunion, when it came, was a joyous one. Raised as an only child, Robin learned that she had several half-siblings, whom she later met and has since seen several times. She says that she has a surer sense of herself since meeting her birth mother. She also has a stronger connection to her adoptive father. "One of the most profoundly important ways to show that you love somebody is to allow them to do what they need to do regardless of your own feelings," she says. "In having the courage to support me in my search, my father's worst fears—that I might become alienated from him—were not realized. In fact, the reunion only affirmed our relationship. You cannot create instant family with people you've just met. The people that I recognize as 'my family' are the people who raised me."

Meet Deborah

There are birth parents among our adoptive parents as well. Deborah is one of them.

Looking at Deborah, a blonde "slip of a girl" dressed in jeans and a T-shirt, one finds it hard to believe that she's been married for twenty-one years. The next bit of information that she divulges is even more astounding. "I have two daughters," she says. "They are twenty-four years apart."

When Deborah was seventeen, she became pregnant. "There was never any question in my family about what I had to do," she says. "My parents simply sent me away to a home for unwed mothers. When the baby was born, it was placed for adoption. I didn't receive any counseling either before or after the birth. I was instructed to tell no one about the experience, to forget about it once it was over, and to get on with my life. My grief was never acknowledged.

"I did not forget about the experience, but I moved on," she recalls. "I attended college and went on to graduate school. I also made a good marriage. My husband Michael and I both had careers that we enjoyed. We lived well, traveled a lot, and managed to accumulate a lot of material things. We had no children. (At the time, we thought it was by choice). Our lifestyle suited us.

"One day," Deborah continues, "I received a phone call from my mother. She sounded quite flustered. 'I've spent days struggling over whether to tell you about this or not,' she said, 'and I just hope I'm doing the right thing.' The news that she then shared was that she had been contacted by an attorney who claimed to represent the daughter I'd given up eighteen years earlier, and who was now seeking information about me. 'Here's the lawyer's phone number,' my mother said. 'What you do with the information is up to you.'

"The first thing Michael and I did was to get in touch with our own lawyer, and pass on the information. I needed to know if the call was legitimate. When he reached the man who had telephoned my mother, our lawyer learned that the young woman, Rachel, had no intention of intruding on my privacy. All she was asking for was a photograph—she wanted to see what I looked like. Further, we were assured, her search was being conducted with the knowledge and support of her adoptive parents."

Deborah's story continues: "I was thrilled that Rachel had made contact. I had wondered about her always, but I never would have searched for her, never would have dared to invade her life. Now she was almost real. There was so much more than a photograph that I wanted to share with her. I asked if it would be all right for me to send her a letter, and was told that it would be fine. The letter led to a phone call, then a meeting, then a relationship . . . not just with Rachel but with her warm, wonderful, and completely accepting parents and their two sons, Rachel's brothers. They have taken us wholeheartedly into their lives. When Rachel was married a year ago, we not only attended the wedding, we were seated up front as members of the immediate family.

"A funny thing happened to Michael and me, however. Meeting Rachel brought out a lot of maternal and paternal feelings in us, while meeting her adoptive family gave us an added sense of appreciation for family. Suddenly, we found ourselves wanting to have a child. Because of our ages, we consulted a doctor who specializes in high-risk pregnancies. It didn't take him long to discover that we had a fertility problem. It also didn't take *us* long to turn to adoption as the answer. It was more like 'Wow, we'll adopt.' And we did.

"Our daughter Alexandra is two years old. She's fantastic, the most wonderful thing to happen to us. Michael and I look at her in wonder. We can't imagine our lives without her. Still, I don't regret having waited so long to enjoy motherhood. I do believe that everything has its time and place. I just wasn't ready for this earlier in my life."

ARE YOU CONSIDERING ADOPTION?
HERE ARE THE QUESTIONS MOST FAMILIES ASK

No matter what their personal experience has been, most men and women come to adoption the same way as did Marie and Ken, the couple who introduced this chapter. They step into the process tentatively . . . afraid to ask questions, afraid to rock the boat. So, I decided, it might be helpful if *I* raised those questions that you, the adoptive applicant, might be concerned about, but afraid to ask. And I thought it would help if I tried to supply the answers, too. So here goes.

Q: How do I know if I am eligible? Who can adopt?
A: The traditional eligibility requirements for adoptive parents have changed in several ways over the past years, largely in response to the definition of an "adoptable child" having expanded to include older children, physically and emotionally challenged youngsters, children of color, brothers and sisters who wish to grow up in the same family. (See chapter 8.) To meet the needs of these children, the definition of an adoptive parent has been expanded as well. Today, for example, social-service agencies placing "special-needs children" are actively recruiting adoptive applicants among single people, experienced parents, older people who may have already raised a first family, and among black and Hispanic community members. The ability to love and commit to a child is the major requirement. In many cases, financial subsidies are available to assist families in meeting the (often extraordinary) needs of the children.

When it comes to placing healthy babies, however, the requirements in most cases are not so elastic. For many infant placements, most agencies will only consider married couples between the ages of twenty-five and forty who have a stable employment income. Some agencies require that the couple have no other children and be able to offer proof of infertility. (At Golden Cradle, as at many other agencies, we do place second children with certain couples who have adopted their first children through us. We feel that they are now part of the Golden Cradle family.)

Adoptive applicants who are unable to meet the criteria set by agencies might be better off exploring either private adoption—in which an attorney or other intermediary brings the applicants together with the birth parents—or investigating a relatively new form of adoption called "identified adoption."

Colloquially, this method has also been referred to as "bring your own birth parent." Here's why: In this form of adoption, it is up to the aspiring adopters to locate a birth parent—through word of mouth or advertisements in various community newspapers—and *then* employ the services of an agency. As in any adoption that it handles, the agency then assumes responsibility for counseling the birth parent, educating the adopters, and doing the home study.

Certainly, I would recommend the identified or private adoption route for single applicants who wish to adopt infants—people like Helen.

Helen and her husband were in the process of adopting when they decided to end their marriage. After her divorce became final, thirty-six-year-old Helen felt that while she had made a bad choice in husbands, she'd made a good choice in deciding to raise a child. She wanted to go ahead with her plan, but the agency she was working with said no. Helen then approached an attorney who specializes in adoption, and learned that her single status was not viewed by him as an obstacle to adopting. Indeed, in Helen's case, it proved to be an asset.

"The birth mother's experiences with men hadn't been good," she explains. "The fact that I was an independent woman who was eager and able to assume the responsibilities of motherhood was what made her select me for her child." Helen not only met her son's birth mother, a nineteen-year-old student, but served as her coach during labor. "It was the most exciting experience of my life," Helen says, adding, "Motherhood is the most rewarding."

Applicants who are older than the maximum age requirements set by agencies also are likely to find private adoption more hospitable. Age has become an important consideration nowadays, when so many applicants are in their late forties or fifties. I see what's been happening in adoption as reflecting changes that have taken place in society as a whole. For one thing, couples are marrying later and then waiting longer to begin planning a family. During the past decade, the attitude seems to have been: career first, children next. (I think that's beginning to change.)

The increase in the age of adoptive applicants is also tied to the greater prevalence of divorce and remarriage in our society. We're finding, for example, that many of the husbands who contact us are older, have been married previously, and even have children from their first marriages. In these cases, it is not the existent children who make them ineligible for consideration by our agency (our focus is on the present marriage); it is the age of the father, who may be in his late forties, early fifties, or older. (Our maximum age is forty-five.) We do try to place babies with parents who are likely to be there for them throughout their growing-up years and, we hope, beyond. We also are aware that most of our birth mothers are unlikely to consider adoptive applicants who are the same age as their parents.

Q: We know that the agency requires adopting couples to have been married for a given time. Technically we're newlyweds, but we've been living together for almost nine years. Can we get some credit for cohabitation?
A: Sure, you can get a lot of credit, but unfortunately not where it counts! To be serious, this question comes up quite often. It's fairly common for men and women who have been living together to finally make up their minds to marry *because* they now want to have children. When conception just doesn't happen, they turn to adoption. They want a baby *soon*. At Golden Cradle, we do not accept the cohabitation years in partial fulfillment of the length-of-marriage requirement. The couples with whom we work must be married at least three years when they apply to us. Although one can never be sure that *any* marriage will last, we think this testifies to a certain kind of stability.

But other agencies—and certainly independent practitioners—are likely to have established different criteria. Ask around. You may be surprised by some of the answers you receive. In one situation that I know of, the couple were living together when they initiated their search for a baby and hired an adoption lawyer. Only after they learned that a placement was imminent did they rush off to find a preacher. Everything worked out smoothly.

Q: We do not actively practice *any* religion. Are we safe to admit it? Or should we rush out and join a church or synagogue?
A: There's no question that religious affiliation is viewed as an asset at certain agencies; some will only work with couples who are church-going members of their faith. Like it or not, that's their prerogative. If you would otherwise qualify at the agency and feel you have a good chance of adopting through them, becoming a dues-paying member of a religious institution might not be such a bad idea. If you are not, don't sweat it. There are other ways to go.

As a matter of practice, a great many social service agencies (Golden Cradle among them) go along with the Standards for Adoption Service established by the Child Welfare League of America, which set forth the proposition that "Lack of religious affiliation or of a religious faith should not be a bar to consideration of any applicant for adoption," further stipulating that " . . . religious background alone should not be the basis for the selection of a family for a child."

That makes a lot of sense to me. It's what I argued years ago when Weezie and I were looking to adopt and were turned away by various agencies because we were of the wrong faith. The way I look at it, love has no labels. I do not think any agency should affix them to parents or children. But—and it's a big but—I do think that the birth parents and their families have a right to express their wish for their child to be raised in their faith. As the adoption standards further point out, "Should birth parents have a preference for a particular religious faith, the agency has the obligation to respect the wishes of the parents in the selection of an adoptive family."

Q: My partner and I are of different faiths. Will that work against us?
A: There's so much intermarriage taking place these days, it's not surprising that this question gets asked a lot. The previous response obtains here as well.

Q: This is my second marriage. Will my divorce be held against us?

A: Most agencies and private adoption practitioners with whom I'm familiar are more concerned about the health and stability of the present relationship than they are about the past. Sure, you're going to be asked about the divorce. You're going to be asked about a lot of things that will probably make you uncomfortable. And if you're like me when I was in your shoes, you'll think it's unfair. Men and women who become parents in the more natural way do not have to justify their right to have and raise children.

It may help to look at it this way. Those of us who are in any way involved in placing children feel our responsibility keenly. We ask questions about the divorce (and about other relationships in your life) because we need to know that you have resolved whatever went wrong and that you feel comfortable, now, in moving forward. We ask questions because, in a sense, a child's fate is in our hands.

Q: Both of us work outside the home. Will I have to quit my job and stay at home after the baby arrives? [Typically, this question is asked by the woman.]
A: Some agencies require that the adoptive mother not work outside the home for at least six months after the adoption. That is not one of our criteria for accepting adoptive applicants, but we do want to make sure that families where both parents plan to continue working have a good child-care plan in place. Having said that, I want to stress again that the choice of adoptive parents is increasingly being made by the birth parents themselves. Many request that the child be placed with an adoptive mother who plans to be at home. In choosing adoption, they want to give the baby something that they themselves are not able to manage at this time.

On the other hand, some birth parents specifically request a family in which both parents work. I have had birth mothers say to me, "I want a two-career family because I've seen too much divorce in my life. If the adoptive parents' marriage breaks up, I want to be sure that the woman will be able to support the children on her own if need be."

This next question is a particularly touchy one.

Q: What if we're still seeing an infertility specialist? Will that be held against us?
A: Some agencies do require assurances from couples that they are done with traveling the infertility route and are now totally committed to adoption as the way to build a family. I don't hold with that. I know that it's possible to honestly pursue adoption while still hoping, in your heart of hearts, for the miracle that will enable you to conceive and carry a child to term. I don't see the point in closing any doors. But I do think you ought to be honest with your agency. I also see nothing wrong with putting your application on hold for a while if you're seeing another doctor or trying another procedure. Quite a few of the couples we work with ask for a breather. They then let us know when it's time to reactivate their application, and we do.

Here's another wrinkle on the same theme.

Q: What if I actually become pregnant while in the process of adopting and I've had a history of miscarriages? Should I risk informing my caseworker of the pregnancy?
A: You better believe you should. I remember one time when a couple came to pick up a newborn baby and the woman was eight months pregnant. Two babies in two months is a bit much for anybody to handle. We spoke with the couple and decided that their adopting at that time would not be in the best interest of either child.

So, if you do become pregnant, tell whomever you're working with. When this situation comes up at Golden Cradle, we keep our fingers crossed for the couple. We hope their dream comes true. If things don't work out as they hope, however, we'll still be there . . . and they can reactivate their application to adopt.

Q: Do we have to own our own home?
A: No.

Q: Is there a minimum income requirement for prospective adoptive parents?

A: Not as such. Items such as your overall income, assets, and debts are reviewed as part of a whole financial picture. In general, those who are in a position to decide on applicants' acceptability are less interested in how much a couple earns than in how well they manage their income. The ability to provide for the needs of the child and the family *is* a major consideration.

Q: How much is this going to cost? Can we afford adoption?
A: At many public agencies, fees for adoption services are charged according to a sliding scale and are dependent on a couple's income. This is true at certain private, not-for-profit agencies as well. It is also true that healthy, adoptable infants are in great demand . . . and that many birth mothers, aware of the situation, are asking for "living expenses" during the pregnancy and "educational aid" thereafter—that is, they are asking for money above and beyond coverage of medical and legal fees involved in the care of the mother and the birth and placement of the baby. (In some states, reimbursing the mother for such additional expenses is acceptable; in other states, it's illegal. As with everything else, when you're not sure about what's kosher and what is not—ask, ask, ask.)

You will find that the cost of adopting differs from one agency to another, one adoption lawyer to another, and often from one case to another (depending on such variables as whether the birth mother had to be flown from one state to another, whether she had an easy pregnancy or the baby was delivered by cesarean section, and so on). At an agency like Golden Cradle, such factors are figured into our costs, and adopting couples are all charged the same fee for our services. As this book is being written, that fee is over seventeen thousand dollars.

I find myself gulping as I put that figure down. Remember, I'm the guy who balked at paying ten thousand dollars about a dozen years ago because it just didn't sound right to me. But I don't have to tell you that the cost of *everything* has skyrocketed in the interim. Let me give you some idea of the financial realities. As the cost of malpractice insurance has catapulted, the fees we are charged by gynecologist/obstetricians have soared to reflect their expenses. Hospital fees have gone up. Counseling fees for the birth parents and educational fees for adoptive couples (almost nonexistent way back then) have gone up. The cost of doing a home study has gone up. The cost of running an office has gone up.

Then there are the several premature babies we deal with each year. At the present time in the New Jersey region, the cost of neonatal intensive care runs at about eighteen hundred dollars a day. Multiply that by thirty—the number of days that the infant is likely to remain in care. That comes to fifty-four thousand dollars, charged to the agency. Yet the cost to the couple adopting that baby is still our standard fee.

The fact is, we could not keep our fees as *low* as they are if it weren't for the fund-raisers we run and the contributions we receive from individuals and especially from the United Way Donor Option Plan, where people designate the nonprofit organization they wish their money to go to. What does a baby cost? At Golden Cradle, we look at it this way. You pay a fee for services; the baby is free. (That's no play on words, believe me.)

Can you afford it? Could you afford the testing and treatments for infertility, the trips to various medical centers that promised new procedures and new hope? You know better than I how much you have extended yourself in the quest to have a child. Only you can decide the answer to this question.

More Questions

Once couples get over the nitty-gritty of whether they qualify to adopt, they begin to ask questions about the birth parents. (I trust that the previous chapter has responded to many of these concerns.) The medical background of the birth parents, the question of what they might be passing down to the child, then becomes a major issue. Here's what our applicants ask.

Q: What do you know about the birth parents' medical history? Can we be sure that the baby we receive will be healthy?

A: Let's take those questions in reverse order. Are you looking for guarantees? There's a saying that you can never be sure about anything except taxes and death. I'll buy that. According to a pediatrician I know, four percent of the population of babies delivered is not going to be perfect. (The child may be born with anything from an extra digit to a congenital abnormality.) The fact is, you'd have no assurances that a baby who'd be born to you would be "perfectly healthy." In this regard, adoption even gives you an advantage. If the baby is born with a serious illness or disabling condition, you can pass. (The agency, of course, will continue to seek a permanent family for that baby.)

In answer to the first question: Generally speaking, you're likely to get a lot more information about the birth mother than you will about the birth father. At Golden Cradle (and I suspect this is true for most other agencies and adoption practitioners), it's not that we dismiss the question of the birth father's background, it's just that the medical histories that we do manage to get are seldom complete. Sometimes a man denies paternity, yet he'll still fill out a medical form. It may be that he wants to protect himself legally, but doesn't want to deny information to the child. Who knows?

We do, however, know a good deal about most birth mothers. We have them fill out extensive medical forms listing every possible medical condition: from harelip or cleft palate through hay fever and other allergies; from asthma through diabetes; from cancer through heart disease; from cerebral palsy through sickle cell anemia; from alcoholism through drug abuse. We ask that information be included on the medical histories of grandparents, parents, brothers, sisters, and any other children born to the birth mother.

We forward this information to the birth mother's obstetrician as a means of securing a thorough medical and birth history on the infant. We also share it with the adopting couple. (If you are not given this information from whomever you approach to help you adopt, ask for it. You have a right to as much information as we have available on the medical background of the child. More importantly, the child has a right to his or her own medical history.)

A note of caution: It can be scary to look at page after page of medical history. Chances are, you *will* see a lot of "yes" answers to the questions. As you go through the documents, this is the kind of information (taken from a sample form) that you're likely to find yourself looking at:

MEDICAL INFORMATION OF BIRTH MOTHER (PG. 2)

MEDICAL CONDITION	YES	WHO?	NO	CAUSE, TREATMENT, MEDICATIONS
9. Tay-Sachs			x	
10. Eczema or other skin condition			x	
11. Hay fever or other allergy	x	SELF		TO GRASS, BEGAN AGE 12, TREATED WITH OVER-THE-COUNTER MEDICATION
12. Drug allergy	x	MOM		TO PENICILLIN, SINCE BIRTH

Now here's a suggestion to help you put the medical information that you receive on your child's birth family in some perspective. Imagine that you are filling out a similar medical form about yourself and your own family, and about your spouse and his or her family. Consider what your own medical histories would look like. Any allergies in your family? Heart attacks? Cancer? What illnesses might a biological child of yours be at risk of inheriting? In short, how perfect are *you*? How might *you* look to a couple considering the adoption of a child whom you might have given birth to?

Also keep in mind the fact that medical information is *not* static. You may be dealing with a very young birth mother . . . suppose a fifteen year old . . . whose parents are about thirty-five . . . whose grandparents are still hale and hardy. Heart disease may not yet have shown up in the family. Cancer may not yet have developed.

What I'd like to impress upon you is that, even given the best of care and the most complete records, the medical history of your child may contain many unknowns. The fact is, you have no way of knowing how long *you'll* be in top-notch form, either.

Face it, adoption is a risk.

Life is a risk.

But I'd sure hate to consider the alternatives.

8

Consider the Children

Let's talk about the children. Chances are that even before you began thinking about adopting as something you might wish to do, somewhere along the line you had already picked up the notion that adoptable children were a scarce commodity. Maybe that kept you from pursuing adoption earlier. Perhaps you felt that nature had already handed you one major rejection, and you weren't prepared to be turned down again. What you have to be absolutely convinced of is that there are children being placed for adoption. So why *not* with you? You ought also to keep in mind that the word "children" is all inclusive. It does not refer solely to "babies."

Let's take some moments to consider the children.

Children With Special Needs

It used to be the case that adoption was sought mostly for healthy, white infants while institutional and foster care became the plan for most other children who were unable to live with their families of origin. Ironically, it took a shortage of adoptable babies to get the adoption establishment to look at the other children in their care, children they had on their foster care caseloads, and to begin to present these waiting children as candidates for adoption. Lo and behold, when applicants learned that these children were available, many came forward to adopt them.

Toddlers proved to be readily placeable. Preschoolers, too, quickly found adoptive parents, as did children with operable disabilities—like having been born with a cleft lip and palate. Subsequently, when older children and youngsters with more serious disabilities were presented as adoptable, families came forward for them, too. What was being discovered, in fact, is that there are men and women in this vast country of ours who are comfortable with adopting a wide range of children.

Some of the children, however, have been able to find acceptance more readily than others. The challenge to find individuals and couples for every child who needs one has resulted in stepped-up efforts to identify permanent families for "children with special needs"—an umbrella term that is generally used to cover all children who are not so easily placeable. The category includes: older children; infants who've been exposed in utero to drugs or alcohol; youngsters challenged by needs of a physical, mental, or emotional nature; and brothers and sisters requiring adoptive parents who are prepared to take on a ready-made family. Half of the waiting children are members of minority groups.

My Feelings About Transracial Adoption

In the world of adoption, the subject of transracial placement has become a hot potato—there's no way to touch it without getting burned. And so most of us *don't* touch it.

While some agencies are willing to place children across racial lines, most will no longer do so as a matter of policy. Pardon the pun but, the way I look at it, this is not a black-and-white issue. I do go along with critics of transracial adoption in a lot of ways. I agree with them that placing a black child in a black family serves to strengthen the youngster's sense of self. *All* children who grow up in adoptive families are likely to struggle with questions of identity at one time or another in their lives, and I have little doubt that transracial adoption may further complicate that issue for them. For that reason alone, I believe that greater efforts must be undertaken to make adoption more accessible to people within the black community so that more of the children who wait can be placed with families of their own race.

While many efforts are being taken in this direction, the results still fall far short of meeting the need. Studies show that although black children represent 14 percent of the child population, they comprise 33 percent of all children needing adoption. There is absolutely no question in my mind that having a child grow up with *no* family to call his or her own is the greatest injustice of all. I can't see how anyone can justify retaining *any* boy or girl in the child-welfare system when that youngster has a chance to grow up with the love and support of a permanent family.

Let's face it, there are many times when life *isn't* fair, and so there may indeed be hard times ahead for children in transracial adoptions. (Almost certainly, there would have been problems for these kids if they'd continued to drift through the foster-care system.) The way I look at it is this: when you come up against life's problems, isn't it better to have parents in your life who will be there to help you face them?

If you are interested in adopting across racial lines (and if you are working with an agency whose policy permits it), you ought to consider the following:

— If you're adopting as a couple, is your partner equally committed to the adoption?
— Do you see adoption as welcoming a child, not taking on a cause?
— Is your decision supported by members of your extended family? I remember once hearing a wise man comment that the success of an adoption (especially of a transracial adoption) rests largely on the attitudes of the grandmother's neighbors. If *they* make an appropriate fuss over the new family member, he went on to explain, chances are good that the grandmother will welcome the child as well, and the adoption will have a greater chance of succeeding. If, on the other hand, the grandmother's neighbors treat

the child's race (or handicapping condition) as something shameful, you may find the grandparent mirroring their attitudes and passing her negative feelings on to the child. While I have no question that the subject is far more complicated than this, I'm equally certain that you can't dismiss the feelings of members of the extended family nor fail to recognize the impact that they're likely to have on the family you form through adoption.

— Are both your neighborhood and network of friends reasonably integrated? Will the child stand out, or be able to feel comfortable in his surroundings? Will the child meet regularly with others of her race?

— Are you willing to "take on" the child's heritage—to learn about black history and black culture so that you can pass the knowledge and pride on to your son or daughter?

As you consider your decision, it may help you to talk to parents who have adopted across racial and cultural lines about what have been their challenges, their frustrations, and their joys. It's a good idea, too, to meet and talk with children who have lived the experience of transracial adoption. I expect you will find that some children adjusted easily to their adoptive families, while others felt caught between two cultures. Listening to the pluses and the minuses, however, can help you determine whether this is something you are ready to do.

Adopting a Child from Another Country

Although special-needs children *are* found among the youngsters adopted from foreign countries, for the most part the foreign children who are adopted by American parents are not categorized as "waiting" since they do not languish in foster homes or group residences in this country. In many cases, however, some of the considerations raised in the previous section apply here as well. Primarily, they are these: Will you be comfortable raising a child who obviously was not born into the family? Does your network of friends include people who reflect the child's race and culture? Are you prepared to learn about the youngster's culture so that you can help instill pride in his or her heritage? And what will the friends of the grandmother say?

Because international adoption has become so popular, and because it is often such a complicated business, you will find further discussion of forming a family in this way in chapter 12.

The Truth About "Unadoptable Children"

It's been said that no child is unadopt*able*, although many children remain unadopt*ed*. I believe that.

There's no question that many of the children who wait for adoptive families are more challenging to raise. But some people who become adoptive parents positively thrive on the challenge. "It makes success all the sweeter when it comes" is how one mother explains the special pleasure she receives from raising her son Alexander. She says, "We had two healthy children when we decided to adopt Alex, who was born with Down's syndrome. Every gain that this gutsy little guy makes is so exciting. For example, when our first two children took their first steps, my husband and I were delighted. But when Alex took his first steps, the whole neighborhood came in and applauded. He brought down the house."

Many agencies specialize in placing children with special needs. In addition, several states require child-welfare agencies to register their waiting children with local, state, regional, and national exchanges that reach a wider audience of potential adoptive parents. These exchanges feature the children's photographs and brief descriptions in loose-leaf books that are made available to child-welfare agencies and adoptive-parent groups which promote the adoption of special-needs youngsters.

At many agencies, couples attending adoption orientation meetings are shown these books. Here is the kind of write-up you might read:

BERNARD—Age 12

Dark-haired, green-eyed Bernard has been in placement for most of his life. During much of that time he kept alive the hope that one day he would be reunited with his parents and family (two big brothers and a younger sister). They would all live "happily ever after."

As he enters his teen years, Bernard is now dealing with the harsh reality that this is not to be. He also is struggling to overcome the terrible memory of an accident that resulted in the death of his foster mother and father, and left him with a mild limp. The emotional scars, however, are far more serious.

Bernard is a good athlete and an avid Red Sox fan. In a class for slow learners, his favorite subject is history. He is expected to be able to do better work, however, once he experiences the security of a permanent family. Bernard will require a lot of patience as he learns to love and trust again. The agency is looking for a two-parent family, but will consider single applicants.

Videotapes of some of the waiting children also may be played. (Reading about a child with a disabling condition can be daunting; seeing what the same child is able to accomplish *in spite of* the condition, on the other hand, can be very encouraging.) It is hoped that couples who are given information about the waiting children will leave these meetings with a heightened awareness of the variety of children who are in need of permanent families, and decide to look into special-needs adoption.

That's what happened to Ted and Harriet.

"Like everyone else we knew who was interested in adopting, we contacted an agency in search of a baby," says Ted, a forty-eight-year-old pharmaceuticals salesman who is married to Harriet, thirty-nine, an advertising account executive. "We were invited to attend an introductory meeting where, we quickly discovered, the focus was entirely on waiting children—handicapped kids, sibling groups, black children for whom the agency was seeking black parents. A number of older children also were featured—kids who'd been in the foster-care system and, for one reason or another, were now being made available for adoption. This was not the kind of meeting we had expected. We'd anticipated hearing about the agency requirements, to find out whether my age would be considered a drawback, and to learn how long the wait was for a healthy white baby.

"On the way home," Ted continues, "I was surprised to hear myself confess to Harriet that I'd never really *liked* babies, that the kids with whom I best related were what I call 'talkable children'—old enough for there to be some give-and-take between us. I also suggested that an older child would be better suited to our lifestyle. We wouldn't have to trade in our friends, who were well past the baby stage, for younger 'playground parents.' While I had no illusions that becoming a first-time parent to an older child would be a piece of cake, I felt that there was something worthwhile about being able to do something for a child who really needed us."

After talking it over and doing some research into older-child adoption, Harriet and Ted returned to the agency where they applied to adopt a girl—preferably one between the ages of six and eleven, they told their caseworker. The child whom they wound up welcoming into their lives turned out to be an eight-year-old boy. Two years later, they can't imagine their family in any other constellation. Like all adoptive parents, they are convinced that fate had a lot to do with it—that their son Paul (and no other) is the child they were meant to have.

The moral of this story is: Don't close off the possibility of adopting a youngster who would no longer qualify as a model for a Gerber baby-food ad, just because of the general expectation that the road to parenthood begins with a baby.

Now here's a different true-life story. (Although I can't quite put my finger on it, I've no doubt there's a moral contained in this one, too.) When Lorna and Ben, both in their early thirties, considered adopting, they spoke about looking for a physically disabled child—someone who would need their care and support. As a young girl, Lorna had been especially close to a young cousin born with spina bifida, a disease involving the spinal cord that often results in neurological impairment, and she knew a good deal about the condition. Most important was the fact that she was comfortable with it, and with the kind of care it required.

The couple applied to their local agency, where they spoke of their wish to be considered for a physically-challenged child. While there, they thumbed through the waiting-child books, expressing interest in several of the featured children.

Their home study went very smoothly. They got along famously with their caseworker and were approved without a hitch. Because they were interested in a child who was already available (not one who had yet to be born), they were not surprised to receive a phone call from the agency within just a few months of being approved. They were *more* than surprised by its message, however. "Congratulations," they heard their worker say. "A healthy, eight-pound, red-haired little boy was born this morning. He's absolutely perfect for you."

It isn't all that unusual for a worker to "take to" a couple and decide what kind of child is best for them—and that is just what happened in this case. As Ben later said, "Lorna and I really were at ease with our decision to adopt a child with a disability. But when the perfect baby was offered to us, we didn't have the guts to say no."

I haven't told this story expecting you to sympathize with Lorna and Ben, but I have included it to illustrate the fact that what others think can have an influence on what you decide and on the family you end up with. If you are unsure of your own feelings, it may help to explore them with your caseworker.

If you want to know what it's like to adopt an older child or a youngster with a physically or mentally disabling condition, it's a good idea to arrange to meet with parents who have chosen to live that experience, and ask them the questions that are on your mind. If the agency cannot link you up with appropriate parents, you may want to get in touch with the North American Council on Adoptable Children (NACAC), an advocacy organization that is largely made up of adoptive parents, many of whom have adopted special-needs children. (See appendix I.)

On the upside: The need to find families for waiting children has led many child-welfare agencies to expand their definition of "who can adopt" to include older applicants (indeed, age and experience frequently are regarded as assets), single adopters, heads of large families, and parents who are themselves handicapped (and may be able to pass their coping skills on to the children). In the past, the costs of care and services were often obstacles to people who might otherwise have adopted a child with special needs. Today, however, adoption assistance is available at the federal and state levels to help parents with the costs involved in meeting the needs of the child.

There are many areas to explore when considering adoption of a special-needs child, among them:

— (If married) Are both partners comfortable with the decision? Actually, I think this question should be asked of all couples deciding to embark on parenthood—whether biologically or by adoption, whether of a healthy infant, older child, or a youngster whose condition requires special care. *Are we both prepared to become parents?* The reason for stressing it here is that the child who joins the adoptive family in this case is likely to require more parental attention from the start. Unless the adoption is truly a joint venture, resentments can set in.
— Do you have a realistic understanding of the needs of the youngster—the child's strengths and limitations?
— Are schools and services available in your community to meet the specific needs of the child?
— Are you prepared to be tested? This is especially important when adopting an older child, someone who is likely to have lived in several foster homes or group homes—perhaps even with an adoptive family—before coming to live with you. Here's what you may be in for. Typically, there may be a honeymoon period, when the youngster is good as gold. Beware . . . it is often followed by a period where all hell breaks loose as the boy or girl begins to test your promises of commitment. Do you think you'll be able to hang in?

   The adoption of an older child has been likened to

a marriage: both sides have to want it and work at it. Those adoptive parents who have managed to get through the tough times say that the resulting relationship with their child is very rewarding.
— Can you count on having the agency's support *after* the child has been placed? Be sure to check into the availability of postadoption services. It's important to know that there's somewhere you can turn when you or the child need advice or assistance.

In short, it's important to do your homework if you want to end up with the kind of child you feel is right for you.

It's "Okay" to Want a Baby

Mind you, there's nothing wrong about reaching a decision that the right child for your family is a healthy baby. While some people (like Harriet and Ted) credit the orientation meetings for expanding their notion of "adoptable child," other couples come away from the meetings with a feeling of resentment that they're being pressured into considering a waiting child.

I understand the feeling, but I also understand the pressure. It's easy sometimes to lose sight of the primary purpose of adoption, which is: to find permanent families for children who need them. Letting people know about the children ("advertising them" is how I look at it, and I think that's a good way to go about it) is the most successful method of locating parents for the children who wait.

But I don't think you should come away from the meetings feeling ashamed because, with so many children waiting for families, you *still* want to adopt a healthy baby. Don't feel guilty. Don't feel that you have to justify your choice. This is, after all, a family you're creating. *Your* family.

It's important for you to do some honest soul-searching about the kind of child you are willing and able to accept parental responsibility for. If the child you envision is a healthy baby, then you must be honest with the social worker about your feelings, even if you're concerned that such candor may hurt your chances with the agency. Remember, Weezie and I once had to make that decision when offered an infant who might later have developed a kidney ailment. In our hearts, we were not prepared to take on a physically-challenged child, and so we said no. Of course we asked ourselves the inevitable question: what if we'd had a child born to us who was not "perfect"? We also were sure of what our answer would be—that we'd accept our responsibility and do the best for our baby. But that's one of the upsides of adoption: you do have some choices. Don't be afraid to express them.

Do use some common sense, however, in expressing those choices. I remember one husband and wife who listed their "criteria" in such detail, it was as if they were placing an order for a customized baby. They asked for a baby of Scotch and English background, one who would have light hair and blue eyes. They further requested that the birth parents be tall, athletic and, in one way or another, involved in music making. Then they announced that they were flexible: they were willing to accept either a boy or girl. Needless to say, I would not work with this couple. I felt that their expectations of adoption were unrealistic, to put it mildly.

Nature vs. Nurture: The Big Question for Adoptive Parents

Realistically, it's important for adoptive parents to be willing to accept difference: that the child may look different from them; that his temperament may be different; that his talents may take him in a different direction. It's important also to recognize that much of what makes your son or daughter special derives from the people who gave him or her life.

Granted, that's not always easy. There may be times when you find it hard to even admit that the birth parents exist. "I feel so close to this child, it's hard to believe she didn't grow in my body" is a statement I've heard from many an adoptive mother. I understand that this is not meant as a negation of the existence of the birth parents. Rather, what the adoptive mother is saying is that the relationship feels so right, it must be natural. I know that feeling.

You may also be tempted to downplay the contributions of the birth parents to what makes your child unique. As one adoptive father expressed it, laughing, "My wife and I tend to take credit for all of our daughter's accomplishments and to lay off any negative attributes to her birth parents. Hence, *of course* she plays the piano well. (Didn't we see to it that she had lessons?) But she absolutely refuses to take to skiing, which my wife and I love, and in spite of the fact that we've given her lessons. ('Her birth parents must not be very well coordinated,' we say.)"

Many people who consider adopting tend to get hung up on this question of nature versus nurture. It is so tempting to think that environmental influences are stronger than genetic ones, and that we can mold a child to fit our expectations. (Let me point out the obvious: such conformity isn't assured by having a child biologically. Just think for a moment: did *you* always go along with your parents' wishes? In what ways have you forged a different path than the one they would have had you follow?)

Although the subject remains controversial, the evidence that is available today seems to be placing more weight on the importance of heredity in human development than on the influence of environment. We know, for example, that physical appearance (such things as coloring, features, and stature) is inherited, as is the likelihood that one will develop certain conditions and diseases that exist in the family of birth. Studies also have shown that much of our intelligence is inherited, and that children are born with predispositions for certain behavior: to be outgoing or easy-going; creative or conforming. Genetics may even account for the use of certain gestures (like speaking with one's hands).

It is important, therefore, for adopting parents to let go of their fantasies about the child they expected to conceive so that they may cherish and nourish the unique qualities of the children they gain through adoption. It is also helpful to keep this in mind: although children may get many of their abilities from their birth parents, environment plays a large role in helping them develop these abilities. Parents who know that a child comes from an artistic background, for example, can do much to encourage his creativity. (On the other hand, you have to be careful not to foist art lessons on the child who is not interested, simply because you know that one of his birth parents was an artist.) Environment offers children the opportunity to develop their innate abilities and to discover new capabilities. Additionally, we would all do well to realize that the making of any individual is much more complex than the sum of the two parts of heredity and environment, that it also involves the indefinable qualities that make each of us uniquely our own person.

That message is brought vividly to life in the personal history related by a woman whom I shall call Cora. Adopted in infancy, Cora grew up in a happy home, married, had a child and, at that point, decided to seek some answers to questions about her identity with which she had long been struggling. With the support of her adoptive parents, she set out to find her birth parents—a search that was ultimately successful.

"When I met my birth mother, I was amazed to discover how many things we have in common," Cora said. "For one thing, we look alike—especially around the eyes and mouth. And our hands . . . our hands are the same shape! I found myself staring at her. I had never met anyone I looked like before. We also have a similar sense of humor. And we both like to do creative work. My adoptive mother, who can't sew a button on, has always marveled at the fact that I love to knit and sew. Well, my birth mother takes her knitting with her wherever she goes. So I guess I came by it honestly.

"But a funny thing happened after I met my birth mother," Cora continued. "I suddenly realized just how much of the person who I've become can be attributed to my adoptive parents. My interest in books, for example. That comes from my dad, who read to me when I was young and who still sends me copies of books he thinks I'd like—and he's generally right. My sense of wanting to do things for people . . . that comes from my mom. In talking with my birth mother, I found myself saying things exactly as my mother—my adoptive mother—would say them: the same words, the same tone of voice. I had never realized how much of her there was in me.

"I also discovered something else after I met my birth parents," Cora went on. "There is a part of who I am that is not attributable to them *or* to my adoptive parents. There's a part, I learned with pleasure, that is uniquely me!"

The way I see it, the fact that adoptees are not clones of either their birth parents or their adoptive parents is what makes parenthood all the more interesting. *Everything* is possible. The fun and the challenge in raising an adopted child is in being privileged to join your son or daughter on this great adventure of growth and self-discovery.

9

Addressing the Openness Issue

The leader of a popular series of workshops for prospective adopters commented recently, "The minute I mention the term *birth mother*, people in the audience become uncomfortable and begin to fidget. There have even been times when a few have gotten up and marched out of the room. That's how hard it is for some people to acknowledge that the child they will eventually take as their own has another set of parents."

Like it or not, anyone interested in adopting in the 1990s can't walk away from today's reality: openness is the most dramatic change to have taken place in adoption in recent times.

It was born of the efforts of adoptees, people like Florence Fisher and Betty Jean Lifton, who insisted on their right to know their origins, and broadened their cause to include all others in their situation. It was carried further by birth parents who were outspoken in favor of the right of adopted children, upon attaining adulthood, to gain access to whatever information about their origins they wanted, including the right of reunion. In a curious partnership, openness was furthered by adoptive parents (especially of special-needs children) who insisted to agencies that they, too, wanted to participate in the making of adoption plans. The adoption establishment, which had been so powerful for so long, was challenged.

All of this has led to a rethinking of adoption and who it's for, and to a strong change of focus—from the agency or other intermediary as the ultimate decision maker (about who shall adopt and what the rules will be) to our newer role as facilitators. In essence, what has happened over the past ten years or so is that the center of control has shifted from the agency or other professional intermediary to the people who are involved in their own family planning—the birth parents and the adoptive parents. And the birth parents have been successfully demanding greater openness.

Before deciding on how you wish to proceed in pursuing adoption, therefore, it's important to take some time to consider the questions of confidentiality and openness. How you resolve to deal with these issues is bound to affect the way you go about adopting. In some cases, it may even determine whether or not your quest will be successful. A note of caution: *Don't make snap judgments. This is one area where it can be especially helpful to listen and learn.*

What You Don't Know Will Hurt You

Some of my own soul-searching on this issue may be instructive. A dozen years ago, questions of openness rarely came up for consideration by those who planned adoption for their children or by those who planned to adopt. Closed adoption (in which the privacy of all the parties is assured) was the rule, and secrecy was the name of the game.

Birth parents who chose adoption were instructed to forget the children they bore and get on with their lives. And adoptive parents? Weezie and I weren't given a platter of choices. The general feeling, as I remember it, was that the less you knew about the child's biological history the better off you were. Later on, this reasoning went, if the child were to ask you questions about "where did I come from," you could look your son or daughter in the eye and honestly answer, "I'm sorry, I don't know." I have to admit that, when I first began investigating adoption, that's the way I felt. It's the what-you-don't-know-won't-hurt-you approach. And I bought it.

Since that time, I have come full circle from accepting confidentiality to advocating openness in adoption. I think that our billboards were an important step in demystifying adoption and taking it public. In a sense, I now view openness as another card in the deck. How much openness? I'm not sure. You see, I'm still learning and, I hope, growing.

When I first got into the business of arranging adoptions, I recommended confidentiality to others—and I found myself being highly criticized by the advocates of opening adoption records. I got chopped up by members of CUB (Concerned United Birthparents) and Adoption Forum (one of many organizations championing the adoptee's right to know his or her origins). They felt that at Golden Cradle we were taking babies from young mothers. They were wrong about that. They had no idea about the kind of options counseling we have always done; the fact that adoption really is the birth parent's decision. But they were right in pressing for greater openness. Had they, and other groups like them, not been so outspoken and persistent, the changes they hoped to create would not have come about.

For one thing, they made it very clear that, although the birth mother does manage to get on with her life after relinquishing her baby, she does not forget. She continues to have a lifelong concern for that baby and its welfare. Agencies with histories longer than Golden Cradle's have been provided with ample proof of this ongoing interest. To offer just one example: during the Vietnam War, adoption agencies reported receiving many calls from birth mothers of sons who would then have been old enough to be eligible for the Army. The women were not seeking reunion with their sons, they assured the agencies. They wanted only to know that the young men were alive and well.

I can certainly sympathize with the birth family's wish to know how the child is faring. To address that concern early on, Golden Cradle requires that its adoptive parents fill out "sharing sheets" for each of the first six months following placement. The sheets record the baby's progress: height, weight, turning over, smiling, sucking. They also share events in the baby's life—describing a party to welcome the baby home or a plane trip to introduce the baby to Grandma. The agency then forwards the sheets (accompanied by a recent photograph of the baby) to the birth family.

This is how a sharing sheet might read:

SIX-MONTH SHARING SHEET

1. Does baby roll from back to stomach? Yes ___ No___
2. Is baby beginning to move about on floor, using legs to push? Yes ___ No___
3. Does baby stand with support? Yes ___ No___

. . .

13. Does baby turn when he/she hears his/her own name? Yes ___ No___
14. Does baby try to imitate facial expressions? Yes ___ No___
15. Is baby disturbed by strangers? Yes ___ No___
16. Does baby play games such as peek-a-boo? Yes ___ No___

. . .

19. Please use this space to make comments.

The space for comments runs several pages in length, and is generally filled with information about what the baby is eating ("He loves carrots, but doesn't do too well with peas"), doing ("She spent the summer splashing in a small backyard pool, and now gets very excited whenever she sees water"), and enjoying ("My husband sings to him, and he just adores it. It calms him down. You know, I never heard my husband sing until this baby came into our lives. Thank you for that.")

When we introduced this means of information sharing, we continued to be careful about keeping all identifying information confidential. The letters were addressed to "Dear Birth Mother" and the child would be referred to as "our baby." Indeed, staff members at Golden Cradle were required to read through each sharing sheet, making sure to "white out" any slips—such as a couple's referring to one another by name or mentioning the baby's real name, writing "Claudia" instead of "she." Nowadays, actual first names of all the parties are used. We came to understand that keeping the names secret serves no useful purpose. There have been no negative results of this change in policy.

Addressing the Openness Issue

As concerns others kinds of openness, we see our task as helping to educate the birth mothers and adoptive applicants to the possibilities—and being supportive of whatever decisions they reach about the kind of ongoing relationship that is right for them. We believe that no one should be pressured into going along with a plan that doesn't *feel* right. We also believe that, in order to reach an *informed* decision, it's important to act on knowledge as well as gut feeling. I hope in this chapter to help you become more knowledgeable about what openness in adoption entails. As I see it, it makes no sense to walk out of the room when the subject comes up. You'd do much better to stay put for a while, to listen, and to learn, so that you can come to a considered decision (not an emotional reaction) about what is right for you and for the child who joins your family.

The Possibilities

There are many forms of openness in adoption. All include some exchange of identifying information between the birth and adoptive families. The possibilities run the gamut, from a one-time sharing of information by letter or phone call . . . to periodic contacts (which are often made through intermediaries) . . . to an actual encounter between the birth parents and adopters (which sometimes occurs, at the birth parents' request, *before* placement) . . . to the birth parent's handing the baby over to the adoptive couple (This is a situation that we've recently begun to encounter; by passing the baby on to the adoptive parents, the birth parent feels—in a sense—that she's truly entitling them to raise the child) . . . to an ongoing relationship among the parties (an actual *open* adoption, sometimes also referred to as a *cooperative* adoption).

First Step: Setting Everyone's Fears to Rest

I don't see how it's possible for the adopting couple to agree to any of the choices that fall under the heading of openness without *first* acknowledging the existence of the other set of parents and *then* learning not to be fearful of them. As we saw in chapter 6 where the "turnaround meeting" was described, simply seeing and listening to actual birth mothers is enough, in many cases, to challenge the notion held by some adoptive applicants that birth parents are to be avoided rather than (somehow) included in the ongoing life of the child. It is enough, at least, to open one's mind to the possibilities.

I also believe that both parties have to be prepared in order to overcome their fears, for *both* the adoptive applicants and the birth parents have fears. Of paramount concern to both, for example, is the fear of rejection. The adoptive parents, who know they are being judged, worry about how they will measure up against other couples whom the birth parents may be considering. The concern is not one-sided, for the birth parent comes to the meeting with a similar anxiety. *What if the adoptive couple doesn't like me?* she wonders. *Will they take it out on my child?* Another thought that makes her uneasy is: *What if I don't like them?*

I look at it like this: if there *is* a mismatch, isn't it better to know that *before* the baby is placed? More than likely, however, the participants in a meeting have been given information about one another before they agree to meet. Chances are, they've spoken on the phone and may even have exchanged letters and photographs. The meeting underscores a feeling they have already developed—the feeling that this match is right.

Fear of envy is another of the qualms that both parties may have about meeting. For the adopting parents, especially the woman, there may be concern about managing a face-to-face encounter with someone who is pregnant, someone who has been able to accomplish what, for her, has been so elusive. For her part, the birth mother is concerned about how, in meeting the adopting parents, she will react to these people who have their life together and are eager to take on the very responsibility—of raising a child—with which she finds herself unable to cope.

In my experience this fear has not turned out to be a problem. For both parties, I have found, envy is replaced by the emotion of gratitude ("that someone else is able to do for me what I cannot accomplish for myself").

Fear of intrusion is yet another consideration that the parties to an adoption often have in common. The adoptive parents may worry that, having met them, the birth mother (perhaps also the birth father and birth grandparents) will want to remain actively involved in the child's life, attending birthday parties and family gatherings, sitting in judgment on how the child is being raised, causing confusion. In fact, we are finding, while contact is generally high in the beginning of an open adoption, more often than not it tends to fall off thereafter. With the passage of time, the birth mother is in a different place. She's gotten on with her life, her job, her personal relationships. She may have married and had another child. It's difficult and even uncomfortable for her to continue the relationship with any intensity.

For the birth parent who shares the fear of intrusion, her apprehension is that the adoptive parents might misinterpret any distancing from the child as a lack of concern, that they might expect more participation from her than she is ready to commit to—certainly at some times in her life more than at others. For some birth mothers, constant reminders of the child work against their being able to resolve the placement and get on with their lives. They need some space.

The best way to deal with fear of intrusion is for the parties to communicate their feelings to one another, as gently but firmly as possible, if the fear turns into a reality. In my experience, it seldom does.

There is also fear of kidnapping. This is the kind of dread that belongs to the adoptive parents alone—the fear that the birth mother will one day reclaim her baby. On that score, all I can pass on to you is what adoptive parents tell me—that meeting the birth parents does not contribute to that fear. On the contrary, it allays it. "*Knowing* Mary (or Lisa or Julie Ann)," they say, "we don't believe she would ever do such a thing to us."

Learning from Others

As in all else involving adoption, I don't think you ought to make decisions about openness in a vacuum. Do some research. To gain information, start by reading. There are many good books that describe the experience. (See suggested reading list, page 203.) It's a good idea, also, to meet with adoptive parents who have experienced some kind of openness, and ask them the questions that are on your mind. What works for others may *not* be right for you, of course, but listening to those who have been there may help you to better define your own capabilities and cutoffs.

Let me introduce you, then, to a couple I'll call Fiona and Fred, and ask them some of the questions that may be on *your* mind.

When they applied to adopt, Fiona and Fred had no intention of meeting the birth mother. They expected to participate in a fairly traditional adoption, and then they were confronted by an atypical situation. There was a young pregnant woman, their caseworker told them, who had expressed interest in their profile (the autobiographies they had written for the agency) but who had set as a condition of placement that she meet the couple before reaching a final decision. They thought about it overnight, and agreed to a meeting.

Q: Were you afraid of the meeting?
Fred: Of course we were afraid—but the question we had to confront was: were we *that* afraid that we weren't willing to meet her and face rejection? We told each other: After all the humiliations we've already been through, what's this?!

Q: Where did the meeting take place?
Fred: At a diner she'd selected near the agency.

Q: Was your caseworker present?
Fiona: No. She offered to join us, but we all felt that would not be necessary.

Q: What stands out for you about the meeting?

Fiona: The fact that the birth mother was taking such care in selecting the couple who would raise her child. As much as she wanted to learn about us, however, she wanted us to understand the circumstances behind her decision to place the child. She'd been working as an au pair, she explained, and had become involved with the husband. She'd left her employer's home early, before the wife could learn of the relationship, and did not feel that she could bring the baby to her parents or raise the child herself. She said she planned to leave town after the birth and asked if we'd be willing to write her via the agency, from time to time, and let her know how the baby was doing. We felt it was the least we could do.

Q: Aren't you afraid that she'll come back someday and reclaim the baby?
Fred: No, because of the process. With the help of the agency, we and the birth mother learned to be comfortable with the realities of openness, including its responsibilities.

Q: Do you have any regrets about having met the birth mother?
Fred and Fiona (in unison): None at all.
Fred: When we tell our child the story of her birth mother's loving decision to make an adoptive plan, she might ask, "How do I know that's so?" And we'll answer, "Because she insisted on meeting us before she would let us have you."

Sometimes the decision to move toward openness is not made before the baby is born or at the time of placement but later. Karen and Peter waited three years before they initiated an open relationship with Elisa, their son Matthew's birth mother. You may be interested in learning how and why the relationship evolved.

Peter tells the story: "Three years ago when we adopted, we didn't know anything about our child's birth parents. We'd fill out our sharing sheets addressed to 'Dear Birth Mother,' as required, and send them off to Golden Cradle, trusting they would reach their destination. When the six-month period ended and we no longer had to communicate with the birth mother, I have to tell you that we felt a certain amount of relief."

"Initially, we didn't like the idea of any openness in adoption," Karen picks up the narrative, "because we didn't want to share the love of our son with a birth family. Peter and I had been trying to conceive for seven years, and this baby was going to be ours!

"Bonding with a child takes place over time," Karen continues. "Peter and I felt much more secure in our roles once Matthew became somewhat independent, could walk and talk, and came to us when he wanted Mommy or Daddy. There was no longer any question in our minds: we were his family. At the same time, we found that we could no longer deny Matthew's receiving the same love and affection from the person who gave him life as he got from us and his other relatives. We phoned the agency and asked them to let the birth mother know that we were willing to meet her and open up the relationship if she agreed to it."

Nineteen-year-old Elisa quickly agreed—although, she admits, she too needed the three-year interval. "It took me that long to accept Matthew as their child," she says. And now? "I visit with the family from time to time. Matthew, who's four, doesn't really understand who I am. I think he thinks of me as a special friend, and in a certain way that is what I hope to be for him. I do know that when Matthew says Mommy, he means Karen. And that's fine."

How have the extended families responded to the open adoption? Karen and Peter's parents remain uncomfortable with the concept of openness. Elisa's parents, too, express caution.

"When they heard that I planned to see Matthew, my father and mother weren't happy about it," Elisa says. "They thought it would be very bad for me and cause me to dwell in the past. On the contrary, what meeting Matthew has done for me is set my anxieties at rest and allow me to move on."

How this story will read ten years from now is, at present,

only a matter of conjecture. Open adoptions are still too new for the jury to be in on how they work out. Nevertheless, says Peter, "I'm glad Karen and I didn't deny ourselves or our son or his birth mother the opportunity to be together."

III

Let's Do It!

10

Working With an Agency

At this point in the book, I'm going to assume that you're no longer stuck in the maze of infertility treatments (although you still may be "trying"), and you're ready to look for a way out. You and your spouse have talked it over, and you're clear about the fact that you both want to have a family. Adopting seems to be the best direction to take in order to reach that goal. Having confronted some of the myths and realities of adoption, you decide to go ahead. The question that looms before you now is *how* to proceed.

BENEFITS OF WORKING WITH AN AGENCY

A good way to begin the process, in my opinion, is by making contact with adoption agencies in your area. Admittedly, I have a bias in favor of working with an agency. While I've heard my share of the adoption horror stories that surround certain agencies and their practices, I still believe that agencies (as a group) are a far cry better than attorneys (as a group) when it comes to adoption. Here's why:

For one thing, most reputable agencies provide counseling to birth parents as well as to adoptive applicants in order to insure that the right decisions are made for the child. Some people view this emphasis on the child as the primary client as a disadvantage of adopting through an agency. I think it is our greatest strength, both for the sake of the child and for your own peace of mind

I under that right now you are focused on *getting a baby*. Once a child is placed in your home, however, you will feel much better knowing that the young woman who bore your son or daughter was given the opportunity to consider her situation, that she was helped to explore the choices available to her, and that she came to a considered and informed decision that placement was right for her and the baby at this time. You will be pleased that the birth family felt secure in placing that baby with you *because* you had met certain qualifications established by the agency and by state regulations to assure (as best as possible) your suitability for parenthood.

As an applicant, once you are involved in the process and able to feel somewhat relaxed about it, you and your spouse will find that the information you gain through counseling, about yourselves as well as about the adoption process, will make you far more comfortable and competent to raise the child who eventually joins your family. I don't want to sound like I'm on a soap box, but I'll take that chance in order to make a point: If you're able to look at the adoption process as an education and *not* as an inquisition, you can (and should) make the counseling process work for you.

Furthermore, decision making at agencies is not dependent on one individual. If you feel that the worker to whom you've been assigned is either inept or unfair, or if you just don't get along, you have a right to ask for a different worker. Don't be afraid to make that request. I know that you may be concerned about the consequences of making waves. Will the agency decide that you're too troublesome to bother with? They may. But if your instincts tell you that things are not going well, then you haven't much to lose anyway, have you?

As a general rule, agencies are likely to keep better records *for a longer time* than are lawyers, doctors, or others who serve as intermediaries between the placing parent and the receiving family. At the least, you can expect them to have a fuller medical history for the birth mother and, when possible, the birth father. Today, a number of agencies are requesting that birth parents provide them with periodic updates of their medical conditions.

To understand why such updating is important, it may help to imagine yourself on a visit to a doctor you haven't seen before. You give the nurse your name, and are handed a form containing questions about your medical history. The answers you put down describe more than your own current state of health. For instance, you might find yourself checking the "yes" column next to heart disease, noting that your father once had a bypass operation. You might answer "yes" next to cancer, adding the explanation that your mother underwent a mastectomy several years earlier. Based on the information that you supply about your medical history, your doctor may order certain tests for you or schedule more frequent checkups than would otherwise be indicated. That's just practicing good medicine.

Now consider the following: If knowledge of your medical background ended with the day you were born, you would have had to leave a lot of answers on the medical form blank. I'm willing to bet that your father's heart condition developed many years after you were an infant, that your mother's breast cancer showed up long after she would have nursed a baby. Your parents' medical records, which are part of *your* medical history, would not be available to you. (Adults who grew up as adopted children report that this kind of scene happens to them all the time . . . and that they find it disturbing).

Ongoing record keeping is important. If you're working with an adoption agency, therefore, it's a good idea to ask if they'll pass along your request for regular medical updates to the birth parents. (If you're adopting independently, I think you should make this same request of your lawyer, but your chances of having the request filled are better with an agency that has the staff to do the necessary follow-up work.) Concerning records, another important point to keep in mind is that agencies are likely to have longer existences than any single practitioner. Even when agencies are forced to close their doors, they are typically required by state regulation to have a plan for what to do with their records.

Potentially, agencies provide good follow-up and post placement services, upon request, to all members of the adoption triad after the child has been placed. Working with an agency enables you to take the long view. Adoption is not a one-time transaction; it's a life. Once the euphoria of the baby's arrival has passed and you begin to settle in as a family, the chances are good that you'll have questions . . . perhaps about how to deal with neighbors whose remarks about your child's adoptive status seem insensitive . . . or, later, whether to tell the nursery school that your child is adopted. You may have originally opted for a closed adoption, and now wish to explore establishing contact with the birth family. You may want advice on handling queries raised by the child, or you may decide that it would be helpful for the youngster to speak to someone outside of your immediate family. An agency is more likely to be able to offer these services than a private practitioner.

For all these reasons, I suggest that you start with an agency. Keep in mind, however, that this advice does not exclude telling everyone you know that you're hoping to adopt or meeting with a lawyer who's been suggested to you. Remember, the key here is to *send out feelers and follow all leads*. As a practical matter, however, you can't be all over the place. If you decide to devote your major energy to working with an agency, here's what you ought to know and do.

First Steps

Compile a list of all agencies in your area that handle adoptions. Nowadays, that's not a very difficult task. Prior to 1982 in the Philadelphia–South Jersey area with which I'm not familiar and in many other parts of the country, if you tried to look up adoption in the classified directory you would only find a reference to "see Social Services." You were supposed to know, for example, that the services performed by an organization calling itself County Children's and Family Society included adoption. (Sometimes you guessed right and sometimes you didn't.)

It took me twenty-two months to convince Bell Telephone and the Reuben H. Donnelly Company, which before the Bell breakup handled all advertisements appearing in the telephone directory, to list adoption separately so that birth parents who wished to discuss placement, and men and women who wished to adopt, would know where to go for the services they needed. Nowadays, therefore, you *will* find adoption agencies listed in your telephone directory.

You will also want to contact the National Adoption Information Clearinghouse (NAIC), which provides information on—and refers people to—local adoption agencies, intercountry adoption agencies, support groups for adoptive and birth family members, crisis pregnancy centers, shelters and residences for pregnant women, and education programs on adoption throughout the United States. Referrals are provided free for up to four states; after that, there is a nominal charge for additional information.

For a broader view of the field, NAIC publishes *The National Adoption Directory*, a state-by-state listing of all agencies doing adoption in America. To obtain a copy, write to the Clearinghouse at: Suite 1275, 1400 Eye Street, NW, Washington, D.C. 20005 or telephone (202) 842-7600. There is a charge for the directory, which lists both public and private adoption agencies.

A public agency is the local branch of your state social service agency. As a rule, public agencies handle only special-needs adoptions—not infant or intercountry adoptions. Private agencies are supported by private funds and are licensed or approved by the state. For the most part, these are the agencies that arrange infant adoptions.

List in hand, start placing phone calls to the agencies. Making the phone calls isn't easy. You feel that you have everything to offer a child, that you ought to be welcomed as a potential parent, and then you run up against a brick wall. It hurts. So steel yourself. I've found it helpful to equate the adoption process to the common cold. For a time, you're going to feel awful, and you have to resign yourself to that. Even at your worst, however, you know that the misery will soon pass and that brighter days are ahead.

Phone one agency after another. If your list includes an agency affiliated with a religious organization and it's one in which you happen to be active, start there. That may be all the connection you need to have your application placed toward the front of the waiting list. If a word from your pastor or rabbi will strengthen your chances, ask your religious leader to speak up . . . to write a letter . . . to make the phone call . . . to intercede in your behalf. Don't be shy about asking. What's the worst that anyone can do—say no?

If you don't have an edge, just start phoning around. The average telephone inquiry lasts about a minute to a minute and a half, I've found. You may get cut off at the pass. Because of long waiting lists, agencies do not always accept new candidates. You may find that the first person you reach says curtly, "Our lists are closed. We aren't taking applications."

Don't write that agency off. From time to time, they will be opening intake. A subsequent phone call might reach them at just the opportune moment. At Golden Cradle, for example, we open intake two times a year for about two months at a time. We do not want to play God. If you call when intake is open and you meet our criteria, you'll receive an application. We look to be inclusive. (I know of one agency that only gives out applications *one day a year*. You have to run down on that day and pick up your application.) If you phone an agency and you're told that intake is closed, ask: "When will you be accepting applications again?" The bottom line is: *Be persistent.*

Suppose you decide to widen your search—a good idea, in my view. You telephone an agency in another state and you hear, "Sorry, we're not doing any out-of-state adoptions." Don't hang up. Ask: "Can you steer me in any other direction?"

If you have a name to drop, *use* it. Connections may not help, but they sure don't hurt.

Write letters. Be brief, but state your case clearly. Explain that you understand that the agency is besieged by people who wish to adopt. Still, you'd appreciate their advice about what, if anything, you can do to encourage the agency to permit you to apply. (Sometimes, I've found, a little humility can go a long way.)

If you do get your foot in a door, should you apply to more than one agency? This is not the kind of response you might expect from someone who's affiliated with an agency, but my answer is *yes*. If you want to adopt an infant, you should register with as many agencies as possible. I remember being told (by an agency that later refused to work with Weezie and me on the basis of religion), "If you're on our list, you can't apply elsewhere." That's nonsense. There will always be couples who are ready and eager to move up on the list, and every baby will find a home. That's the important thing to keep in mind. Do be prepared, however, to compensate the agency for the time they may have invested on your case. That's only fair.

WHAT TO LOOK FOR IN AN AGENCY

People who apply to adopt are generally too petrified to ask questions of the agency. They worry: *What if we ask the wrong ones—will that act as a black mark against us?* Invited to a group meeting, new applicants vie for seats in the back of the room—the more inconspicuous they can be, the better. They're afraid even to look sideways. My advice: *relax*.

Just as the agency will ask questions of you, keep in mind that you have a *right* to ask questions about the agency. You probably won't want or need to raise all of the following questions. On the other hand, several may be very important to you.

- Is the agency licensed or certified by the state?
- Does the agency have an ongoing educational program for its staff? Are they specifically trained in facilitating adoptions?
- How many children did the agency place with families over the past five years? You're interested in finding out if adoption is an active, ongoing program at this agency or only a sometime thing.

— How many applicants do they accept each year?
— What is the average wait for a baby? The key word here is "average." Understand, there are no guarantees. Some couples luck out and get "chosen" by birth parents early on. Sometimes, a birth mother may select a couple but then change her mind about placing the baby. The couple's application then goes back into the active file. Keep in mind that a couple cannot be selected by the birth family nor matched with a child until the home study is complete. I'll talk about the home study later on in this chapter.
— Are the agency's programs geared to finding families for babies, older children, youngsters with special needs, or to intercountry adoption? Many agencies specialize, and, depending on the kind of child you're interested in, you may better your chances by working with one agency over another.
— Does the agency have a religious orientation, and, if so, will they work with couples whose faith is different from theirs? Will they work with applicants who have *no* religious affiliation?
— Does the agency have a philosophy of adoption that guides its practice? For example, is there a strong emphasis on confidentiality? Or do its programs encourage openness, or even insist on it? As the previous chapter makes clear, how *you* feel about these issues can have a lot to do with how comfortable you'll be in working with a given agency. At Golden Cradle, for example, applicants must agree to house an expectant birth mother should the need arise. (Remember, this is not the birth mother of the child they'll end up adopting.) I know of many couples who will not apply to our agency because they are unwilling to go along with this request. They go elsewhere. I think that's honest. It's a lot better than saying yes to every request the agency makes, and feeling uneasy or compromised when the time comes for you to deliver on the promises.

Working With an Agency

— What are the agency's eligibility requirements? Most agencies have established certain criteria around such issues as residency, age of adopters, length of marriage, previous marital history, health, proof of infertility. If you find that you meet most but not all of the qualifications, don't take yourself out of the picture. Ask the agency if there's any flexibility about enforcing their requirements. If you do not meet one of their standards, will you be allowed to plead your case?

— What is the screening and evaluation process like? Are the results of the agency's assessment shared with applicants? What would lead a couple to be rejected? (I'll have more to say about this further on.)

— Will the agency link you up with others who are in the process of adopting? It's a good idea for an agency to have a buddy system that encourages applicants to call one another with questions that they may feel uncomfortable discussing with their social worker. At Golden Cradle, our small group meetings are set up to include couples who live in roughly the same geographic area, so that they will be able to create friendships and call upon one another. We have learned that this is important. Even if you choose to adopt through an independent practitioner, I recommend that you ask him or her for names of other couples whom you can contact. Believe me, it helps.

— What is the screening process for birth parents?

— What services are made available to them? Are they counseled as to their options during the pregnancy, provided with medical care and residential assistance?

— What kinds of information are included in the medical history of the birth families? Are there provisions for update? What's happening out there with drugs is making the whole adoption scene more frightening nowadays, and the work more difficult. It falls to

an agency to do some screening, but policies on AIDS testing differ among agencies. Ask your agency to explain how they are handling this situation.
— How does the agency make a match? What say, if any, do the birth parents have in choosing the adoptive parents? What input, if any, can the adoptive parents have?
— Ask about disruptions. Has the agency experienced many disrupted placements, and, if so, how have they been handled? Although a disrupted adoption—one in which the birth parent reappears after placement and reclaims her child—is more feared than experienced, it does happen. Remember, adoption is a risk. But what does the agency see as its responsibility if disruption takes place? At Golden Cradle, for example, our disruption rate is less than 2 percent. That doesn't mean very much to the families that have had a child removed from their homes, I know. For them, it was 100 percent. Disruption is *always* painful. You can't ever replace a child. The couple needs time to grieve. But in each case that we've had, another child was placed with the couple subsequently.
— What are the fees to adopters? What services do they cover? Are there any hidden costs? Agencies structure their fees in different ways. Some agencies set their fees on a sliding scale, determined by the adopters' ability to pay. At Golden Cradle, on the other hand, we charge the same fee to all. It covers all services, including: adoption education; birth parent counseling; any transportation costs for the birth mother; medical care; termination of parental rights. Other agencies may have a set fee for certain services, then tack on the costs of medical and/or legal services. Still others may increase the fee if extraordinary medical expenses are incurred. I've even heard of agencies that charge extra if there are twins! And of agencies that will tell you that there is *no* fee for adoption—that only a donation is required. But

how much is a couple expected to "donate"? If you're applying to adopt, you should request and receive detailed information on fees *in writing*. I'll go even further. I would insist on it.
— Regarding fees, applicants should also ask, "What portion of the money is nonrefundable if we fail to go through with the adoption—for example, if we find out we're expecting, receive a baby through another source, or if we are rejected? Why?" Advice about fees: some part of adoption costs may be covered by company insurance plans. Check to see if this applies in your case.

If you are uncomfortable with the answers you receive, or if you just don't feel right about the way the agency conducts its business, you can go further. To find out whether any complaints have been lodged against an adoption agency, check with the agency in your state that regulates adoptions. Call the Better Business Bureau. The point of all of this is: Don't just accept an agency because it has accepted your application.

MOVING RIGHT ALONG

The Home Study Process

Let's suppose that the agency has reviewed your application and accepted you as a client, that your questions have been satisfactorily answered, and that both you and the agency are ready to move ahead. What happens now?

At this time, the preplacement or "home study" procedures are set in motion. I'd like to clarify one thing at the outset: what we're talking about here is *not* a study of your home. It is an evaluation of you as a prospective adoptive family, and of the physical and emotional environment into which a child would be placed. It is also a preparation for adoptive parenthood. Although all states require that there be a home visit, the agency's assessment of you (and yours of the agency) occurs as a kind of continuum, which may take place in different settings: in your home, in meetings at the agency, and even in periodic phone calls between the adopting couple and the caseworker.

It makes a lot of sense, doesn't it? Yet just the *thought* of being involved in a home study can send shivers up the spines of men and women who would otherwise feel no anxiety about bearding the lion in his lair. This sense of foreboding is brought about by the suspicion that every corner of your life is about to be looked into. (No doubt you're already thinking, *I'd better sweep those corners*.) There's no use in my telling you that it's foolish to be so concerned. I know that won't make the anxiety go away. You may find it helpful, however, to have your fears replaced by facts—to be given a description, in somewhat general terms, of what a home study will be like. I'll try to do that here.

The adoption qualification process differs from state to state and from agency to agency. You can be certain of this, however: wherever you live and whichever agency you work with, there will be meetings to attend, tests to take, and a seemingly interminable number of forms for you to fill out. There's no getting around it—the process of adopting requires time, dedication, and forbearance. It can (and at times it probably will) be frustrating for you. It can also (and I hope that it will) be illuminating for you.

You will have to gather papers: marriage license; divorce decrees; death certificates (from a former marriage, where applicable); military discharge papers; tax returns; life insurance policies; medical forms on husband and wife; medical forms on other children living in the home; color photographs of the two of you and, perhaps, of your home. At Golden Cradle, we also require couples to submit a certificate attesting to the fact that adopting couples have taken a course in infant CPR (cardiac pulmonary resuscitation). This is not a state regulation or requirement, although I wish it were. I could show you letters from grateful parents whose children's lives have been saved because we required the parents to take an infant CPR course. Thank God I don't have letters from parents who didn't take the course but wish they had!

Screening requirements also include a check for criminal records, as well as personal and professional references. Some agencies (Golden Cradle among them) include a standard psychological evaluation procedure as part of the adoption process. This test has proven helpful in highlighting areas that require further discussion with some of the applicants. In addition, we ask each of the partners to submit fairly extensive autobiographies, beginning with their childhoods and covering such topics as their relationships with parents and other family members. We ask, "In what ways would you hope to be like your parents *as* a parent? What things would you hope to do differently?" We'd like the autobiography to include information about courtship and marriage, about the impact of childlessness on the individual and the couple, and about feelings concerning infertility.

The autobiography requires applicants to move from the past to expectations for the future. It covers such ground as, "What type of child would you prefer?" and "How do you plan to discipline your child?" We are careful to note that New Jersey state regulation requires that all prospective adoptive parents abide by a policy of *no corporal punishment*. If you believe that a quick swat on the backside never hurt anyone, don't write "I would never hit my child," knowing that you're very likely to do so. Instead, *talk* about your feelings with your caseworker. She will help you to develop other effective means of discipline.

The bottom line here is: be honest. For one thing, lies have a way of coming out. For another, you don't want to present yourself as a saint. Caseworkers are savvy to the fact that people who seem too good to be true generally are.

Not all agencies ask applicants to submit their autobiographies. In Golden Cradle's experience, however, it is one of the primary ways that an agency has of getting to know a couple. We are not looking for literary style, but for a realistic picture of experiences, feelings, and relations that have made you the person you are. The clearer the picture that emerges, the better able we are to effect an appropriate match—bringing together adoptive parents with birth parents who share similar interests and abilities.

For many applicants, working on their autobiographies leads to greater insights about how they see themselves as individuals and as a family. It can be an eye-opening experience, helping each partner to see clearly whether he or she is really comfortable with adopting or is just going along with the idea.

The home visit: *Here's the scene that most probably exists in your mind's eye: It is midafternoon. You're at home, pretending that this is a typical day in the life of your family. (Actually, everyone* knows *it's not a typical day, because both of you are at home—and this is a work day!) There's a knock at your door. In walks the social worker. Her grey hair is pulled back in a bun. She wears white gloves. (The better to check for dust.) After greetings are exchanged, she walks across your just-vacuumed carpet and takes a seat on your recently fluffed-up sofa, while you struggle to decide whether it will look better for you to sit next to your spouse, or more casually, across the room in your easy chair. Then the questions begin. . . .*

Actually, our social workers report they typically do find vacuum cleaner marks on the carpets in the homes when they visit. It's understandable—they know that the family is eager to make a good impression. "One of the good things about seeing couples in their home is that they're generally more relaxed," says Joyce Block, supervisor of the Couple's Department at Golden Cradle. (Note: no grey bun or white gloves.) "They're on their own turf, and therefore feel that they have some control over the situation—if only by straightening the house in order to get ready for the meeting."

She goes on: "But the emphasis here is the same as in meetings with the applicants that are held at the agency: to continue the process of information sharing and assessment. Sure, when we visit the home we take a ten-minute tour of the premises. We make note of the layout, the back yard (whether there is room to play, whether it is safe). We ask about schools in the area. What community resources will be available to you and your child? We also make sure that there are the required smoke detectors and fire extinguishers. But those are really the frills. We're not there to make judgments on the décor or to look for dust in hidden corners. While we want to make sure that the environment is safe, the essential part of this meeting is getting to know the couple and to see them as potential parents. I can't separate for you what goes on in the couple's home from what takes place in the agency's office. It's all part of the process."

"What Issues Might Preclude Our Being Accepted?"

Sometimes, at Golden Cradle meetings, this question is asked gingerly. Often it remains unspoken. But it is always there, I know, so let me reassure you. Couples seldom "fail" their home studies. Once an agency agrees to work with you, they're on your side. They want to be able to effect a successful adoption.

Their primary concern, however, is that the child be placed in a safe and loving environment. Keeping that goal in mind, you will understand at once the reasons for rejecting certain applicants. They include:

— *existence of a criminal record* (being convicted for something serious, not just a batch of speeding tickets).
— *documentation of child abuse.*
— *failure to meet child-support obligations.*
— *proof of substance abuse.* We don't turn away applicants for having tried marijuana while in college. *Abuse* is the key word here.
— *presence of a serious medical condition* that affects the applicant's normal life span or ability to care for a child.
— *marital strife.* This need not lead to automatic rejection. There have been cases where we learned that the couple was already in the divorce courts, and that one partner was going along with the adoption as a favor to the other, who would raise the child as a single parent. Now *that* is cause for rejection. Where the husband and wife are just going through a tough time, however, we'd be more likely to suggest marital therapy, and put the adoption on hold while they attempt to work out their problems.

There are other reasons for having applicants go on hold. Among them:

- *job-related problems*. You may be changing jobs or you may have lost a job. At any rate, this is not the time to add the pressure of a new child.
- *medical problems*. An accident or temporary illness may make it difficult for you to care for a baby at this time. When the situation improves, your application can be reactivated.
- *pregnancy*. At first glance, this sure looks like reason enough for rejection. But suppose a couple has had a history of precarious pregnancies, that they have experienced one miscarriage or stillbirth after another. Doesn't it make more sense (and isn't it kinder) to place that couple's application on hold while they await the outcome of the current pregnancy?
- *ambivalence about adopting at this time*. The script goes something like this: you've heard that infant adoption takes years, so you fill out an application before you've completed all of the fertility procedures. Suppose, for example, that you decided to go through three in vitro procedures, and you've only completed one. You can put *yourself* on hold. That is one of the luxuries of adoption, the luxury of timing.

Being honest about your circumstances (whether it's job loss, marital difficulties, or the wish to continue with infertility treatments) will not lead an agency to reject you. Believe me, it takes a lot of work to reject someone.

Postplacement Supervision

The role of the agency does not end with the home study or with placement of the child in your home. The agency has an obligation to supervise the placement until the adoption is finalized. Typically, supervision will take the form of several visits to your home to see how you and the baby are adjusting. Please don't start fluffing up the sofa pillows or scrubbing the nursery down with Lysol. With the stresses and strains that come with having a new baby, you're certainly entitled to have dishes piled in the sink.

The visits are required by law. They are made to ensure that all is going well. But don't look at them as if someone is coming to check up on you. Rather, think of the visiting caseworker as a friend who is coming by to check *in* on you, to help you over some of the rough spots.

Once finalization takes place, it's generally up to you to contact the agency when questions or concerns arise. Most agencies will include you on their mailing lists, however, and let you know about any postplacement services and educational seminars they have scheduled. Take advantage of the opportunity to attend the workshops. Raising children, biological *or* adopted, is a lifelong learning experience—one in which, I've discovered, we parents need all the help we can get.

Identified Adoption

In recent years, many agencies have begun to offer another kind of adoption service to interested members of the community: it's "identified adoption" (sometimes also referred to as "designated" or "cooperative" adoption). It differs from the more typical agency-facilitated adoptions in that the agency no longer plays the role of matchmaker, linking adopting parents to a child in need of placement. In identified adoption, the adopting parents (or someone acting on their behalf) make the contact with a birth parent willing to consider adoption. The couple *then* contracts to use an agency's counseling, home study, and adoption preparation services.

If the parties live in different states, the agency approached by the adopting couple may coordinate services and paperwork with a second agency located in the home state of the birth parent. Identified adoption has answered a particular need in states which have outlawed independent placements arranged through a third party or which require that a home study be conducted by a licensed agency *prior to* an independent placement.

Darcy and Pete used an agency for an identified adoption. Here's how they happened to go this route. The first thing this couple did, once they made up their minds to adopt, was to follow rule number one: "Tell everyone you know." Several months went by while they pursued one lead after another. Then, on a weekday evening, the phone rang in their apartment. It was a long-distance call from North Carolina. The caller, a former college roommate of Darcy's, sounded excited. "A woman in my office recently learned that her daughter, a teenager living at home, is pregnant—not just pregnant, but in her seventh month," Darcy's friend said. "The mother is beside herself. She says the family has discussed the matter, and their only solution is adoption. That's when I told her about you. Interested?"

The couple was interested. They called and spoke to the birth mother and her parents, telling the family about themselves and their wish to adopt. "If you decide to place your baby," Darcy remembers saying to the birth mother, "I hope it will be with us." Several conversations later, the birth mother agreed.

Not too long before these calls took place, Darcy and Pete had been to an informational meeting at an adoption agency where identified adoption had been discussed as one of the options available to couples. Now they contacted the agency, and arranged to use its services. The agency counseled the couple *and* the birth mother (who came north to await the birth), did a home study, secured the necessary releases once the baby was born, and then placed the child with the couple who'd been "designated" by the birth mother. Pete says, "Darcy and I like knowing that we didn't just take advantage of an opportunity that came along, but that our birth mother was able to receive counseling. We feel that it was her consideration, not her desperation, that made it possible for us to become parents to our son. The difference is important."

Identified adoption is not synonymous with open adoption. The parties do not have to meet or exchange identifying information, although conditions for openness might certainly be included in their agreement. The upside of this form of adoption is that it enables couples to be more aggressive in locating a baby and, if successful, it often shortens the process for them. The potential downside is that identified adoption can end up being very expensive, since adoptive parents can find themselves paying fees to the agency as well as covering travel expenses for the birth mother, doctor and hospital expenses, and even living expenses for the birth mother while she awaits the baby's birth. If she then changes her mind, much of that money may not be recoverable. In addition, there is the potential emotional toll one pays *if* the birth parent has been identified and later changes her mind about placement. In more traditional agency adoptions, families are usually contacted only after a child is born and ready to be placed, thus sparing them knowledge that a birth is imminent and any attendant disappointment if the birth parent changes her mind. Of course, there also is emotional risk in certain open adoptions, even those arranged by agencies, where the parties meet before a baby is born.

In short, there is no sure-fire way to adopt a baby. There's only the certainty you must have that there *is* a baby for you. Working with an agency is one way to reach that goal. As the following chapter makes clear, pursuing independent adoption is another.

11

Pursuing an Independent Adoption

Adoptions that are not arranged through an agency are referred to as either "independent" or "private" adoptions. In fact, most private adoptions are made by relatives, such as when a stepparent adopts his or her spouse's child or when parental rights and obligations for a youngster are legally transferred from the birth parents to grandparents or perhaps to an aunt or uncle. In the context of this book, however, independent adoption refers to those nonrelative adoptions that are directly arranged between the adoptive parents and the birth parents, or through an intermediary—most often an attorney.

Because independent adoption is often less restrictive and speedier than adoptions arranged through an agency, it can be particularly appealing to single applicants seeking to adopt healthy infants; to mature couples where one or both partners have passed the age limits set by certain agencies; to couples who already are parents and now seek to enlarge their families through adoption; or in situations where (for a variety of reasons) time is of the essence.

There's no question that, in recent years, the number of independent adoptions has been growing. Agencies have to accept some responsibility for this development, it seems to me. When birth parents were made to feel as if they were being interrogated instead of interviewed, when they were given little or no say in planning for the placement of their baby, they learned to go elsewhere. When adoption hopefuls get turned away in droves, when their names are placed on lists and they are told that the wait for a healthy baby may take "anywhere from two to seven years," people are bound to seek other means of attaining their heart's desire. I don't blame them.

I also believe that the growth in independent adoption reflects the increase in age and achievement of people seeking to adopt. As a recent *New York Times* report on independent adoption pointed out, "More often than not, the new parents are college-educated, urban residents in their thirties, securely married, well organized, and accustomed to directing their own lives." Going the independent route appears to offer them more control. That's an upside. As you will see, it also is likely to involve more work, more money, and more risk. Those who have adopted successfully via this method feel strongly that all the effort (in some cases, even some early disappointment) was worth it. When the end result is creating a family, who will disagree?

Learn What's Legal

If you're considering adopting a child independently, your first task is to learn about the laws in your state that will govern your actions. In a large number of states, for example, independent adoption is relatively unrestricted. Other states—Connecticut, New Jersey, North Dakota, and Virginia among them—ban placements arranged through a private intermediary but permit a birth parent to place her child *directly* with adoptive parents of her choosing. And in still other states—like Delaware and Michigan—independent adoptions by persons unrelated to the child are outlawed completely. (If you are negotiating an adoption with a birth mother who makes her home in a different state from yours, it's important to find out what's legal in that other state too. You also will want to look into whether you're required to establish residency in the birth mother's home state as a prerequisite to adopting or whether an expectant mother can travel to your state and have the baby there.)

Even where independent adoption is legal, rules governing the financial aspects of adoption vary from state to state. You need to know what you're allowed to pay for (generally, it's okay to cover all of the birth mother's medical expenses that are deemed *reasonable* by the state) and which requests for payment you must turn down. I've known situations in which the birth parents or their families have called and demanded money above and beyond their actual expenses. It may hurt to turn a prospective adoptive situation down, but you must do it. In other cases, the generosity of your own spirit will lead you to want to make an offer—say, to contribute to the birth mother's schooling or career training or to give her the gift of a vacation after the baby is born. Again (and I just can't stress this strongly enough), you have to follow the law and not your heart.

Another issue that could place your independent adoption in jeopardy is ignorance of the rights of the birth father. Not so very long ago, birth fathers were virtually disregarded when it came to placing a baby. Typically, it was the birth mother alone who was identified on the original birth certificate. The space for the birth father's name was filled in "Unknown." Since the U.S. Supreme Court decision in *Stanley v. Illinois* (affirming the rights of birth fathers), however, courts in most states have required that every legal effort be made to locate the birth father and obtain his consent to placing the child for adoption or to terminate his parental rights.

If you have located a birth mother on your own and are going ahead with the adoption plan, you cannot neglect to satisfy this condition. There is far more at risk here than the adoption's not going through. It's possible for a birth father who has not been notified about the birth or told about a pending adoption to have the case reopened and establish a legal claim to his baby. If you're working with an attorney who specializes in adoption, he or she should be able to advise you. If questions remain, or if you're arranging an adoption on your own and are unsure of the law, call your state department of social services. Find out just what the requirements are, and make sure that you comply with them.

Understanding the Difference Between "Grey" and "Black"

While on the subject of what's legal and what's not, I'd like to get the matter of black-market adoptions out in the open, since so many people jump to the conclusion that if an adoption is done privately there must be something about it that's unethical at best, and illegal at worst. This perception has been aided by the fact that, for a long time, *all* nonagency adoptions were referred to as "grey market," lending strength to the suspicion that there had to be *something* in the process of private adoption that was not open and aboveboard (in other words, *white*). Fortunately, the term "grey market" has fallen into disfavor lately.

Black-market adoption is another matter entirely. Black-market adoption involves the buying and selling of a child. It involves the paying of money outside of the standard fees for services rendered. It also involves using an intermediary in states where that is prohibited. It *is* illegal, and I advise you not to become involved in it, no matter how tempting the "deal" might sound. I just don't hold with trafficking in babies.

Still, you might find yourself in a situation where you're just not sure if things are on the up-and-up or not. The line between what's legitimate and what's unlawful isn't always so clear. For example, you know that you're permitted (one might even say "expected") to pay medical expenses incurred by the birth mother in connection with the pregnancy, but what if she asks you to pay for having her tubes tied after the baby is born? Is that legal? Or, you know that, in the state in which you live, you may cover housing and food expenses for the mother while she awaits the birth of the child, but one day you receive a bill for payments on her car. What do you do?

Answer: Don't wing this on your own. Once again, my advice to you is to consult a lawyer who is familiar with adoption law, or contact the state department of social services whenever you have any question about what's permitted and what's not.

Supposing you have questions about the policies and practices of the intermediary you've chosen to work with? Don't hesitate to quell your own doubts. If you think the bill for services is excessive, contact your local bar association and ask about the range of fees charged by attorneys in your community for handling an adoption. Similarly, the state medical association should be able to give you some idea of reasonable costs for a normal pregnancy and delivery.

Speaking with parents who've recently adopted is equally informative in establishing some guidelines about which fees fall within the realm of reason and which do not. *And go with your gut.* Believe me, you will *know* when a situation sounds suspicious. Are you being asked to pay a lot of money—half by check and half in cash? Do you have to pick the baby up in some out-of-the-way location? A good rule to go by is this: If the situation feels fishy, it probably is. Don't be afraid to say no.

There are many legitimate ways to pursue an independent adoption. Let's look at what the process is likely to entail.

DOING IT YOURSELF

"Contacts" is the name of this game. Either you have them—you know of someone who is about to have a baby and intends to place the child; you know of a doctor or other professional who has access to birth mothers—or you go out and look for them. How to do that? Start with the simplest and most direct method: *tell everyone you know, beginning with your mother.*

That's the way that Deena and Stuart came to be parents to their beautiful daughter Ilana. After three years of undergoing tests and procedures to treat infertility, Deena and Stuart resolved to adopt. Deena told her mother who immediately sprang to action, reaching out to any and every person she could think of. The name of her rabbi headed the list. As fate would have it, when Deena's mother phoned the rabbi he told her he had recently been approached by another mother who, like herself, had a daughter in need of assistance. In this case, the daughter in question was single, still in high school, and expecting. The family had been seeking a residence where the teenager could live while awaiting the birth of her baby, who would then be placed for adoption. The rabbi had been able to help them.

Perhaps a match could be made, he told Deena's mother. He put the two families in touch with one another and, four months later when the baby was born, Deena and Stuart became proud parents by adoption. The cost to them? Only medical and legal fees. Amid all of the anxiety that surrounds the search for an adoptable baby, we sometimes lose sight of the fact that such simple and direct private arrangements are possible. They do happen.

Prepare a Resumé

Another way to orchestrate an adoption on your own is to prepare a resumé, much as you would if you were trying to sell yourself to a potential employer, except that in this case you're going to stress your human qualities instead of your work experience.

Begin by introducing yourselves: names of husband and wife (if a married couple), ages, length and strength of marriage. In your own words, state your interest in adopting. Be very clear about how much it would mean to both of you to have a child. That's paragraph number one.

What follows is pretty much up to you. More than likely, your resumé will include information about your work, education, and hobbies. If religion is an important part of your life, be clear about that. You'll want to describe your home and community, perhaps also the families in which you were raised (to give the person reading your resumé some idea of how important family life is to you). Describe the kind of life you lead now, and what you do in your leisure time. It sometimes helps to create a verbal image: "A special day for the two of us would be . . . "

Enclose a color photograph of husband and wife. You may also wish to include a snapshot of your home—or of your pet, if you think that will help. And be sure to put down an address or phone number at which you can be reached. (The subject of phone numbers is discussed later in this chapter.)

As you write your resumé, keep in mind that your ultimate audience is the birth mother. She's the one who will be making the selection. If you are willing to speak or meet with her, say so. If you're unsure about how much openness you can handle, don't introduce the subject here.

Maureen and Kevin's search for an adoptable baby had been unsuccessful until they read about "the resumé method" in a national magazine and decided to try it. After completing their write-up and including a photograph which had them posed with their Irish setter before the fireplace in their living room, they followed the article's instructions, creating a list of friends and acquaintances who live in the South and Southwest. They added the names of friends who lived and taught in college towns, thinking that these areas might also be good for contacts.

"Look through your college alumni directories," the article had advised, and so they did. "I felt uncomfortable about sending such a personal letter to people I'd hardly said a word to in college . . . some names I couldn't even connect with faces . . . but then I reminded myself that this was all for a good cause, and I mailed out the letters," says Maureen.

The cover letters basically reiterated the information contained in the resumé, at least the part about length of marriage and the quest for a healthy baby to adopt, and asked the recipients to please forward the resumé to anyone—their doctor, lawyer, religious leader, head of a local civic organization—who might be able to help. "We mailed out forty-seven copies of the resumé," Maureen remembers, "and we prayed.

"The first responses we got were from old school friends who said they had been surprised to hear from us, promised to pass the resumés on, and wished us well," she continues. "We also heard from someone who said she was a nurse and wanted to know how much we were willing to pay for putting us in touch with a birth mother. We told her we weren't interested. Then, about five months after we sent out the letters, we received *the* call we'd been waiting for. It was from a high school guidance counselor who was a bridge partner of a distant cousin to whom we had written. There was a student in her school, she told us, who was expecting a baby and was due any day. The caller wanted to know if we were still looking for a child, and if she ought to pass our name along to the girl and her family. It was a good family, she added. We asked her to please get in touch with them right away."

The following morning, Kevin and Maureen heard from the mother of the young woman who was expecting. They asked about the circumstances of the pregnancy, the health of her daughter, and the medical care the young woman had been receiving. They asked to speak to her obstetrician, who assured them that everything looked good. Next, they phoned a lawyer who had been highly recommended by friends, and asked him to manage payments to the doctor and hospital and to take care of all legal requirements, including arrangements for a home study. In two weeks, when the birth mother went into labor, they received a phone call. Maureen flew south to pick up her son the following day.

What About Advertising?

You may have seen the ads in local newspapers. With some variation, here's how they read:

> ADOPTION—Happily married couple unable to have child desires infant to care for, love, educate—and make our life complete. Legal/confidential. Expenses paid. Call (area code) 123-4567 collect.

Another sample:

> LET'S HELP EACH OTHER—Successful businessman and stay-at-home wife love children but cannot have one. We will help you with expenses, provide your infant with love, fine education, secure home in rural setting, doting relatives. Please call Judy and Bill collect at (area code) 123-4567.

In much the same way that Maureen and Kevin orchestrated their resumé campaign, people wishing to make contact with a birth mother can choose to write ads such as these, placing them in selected newspapers in various sections of the country.

You may balk at doing this. You may feel very uncomfortable about the notion of advertising for a baby. I have to admit that I have mixed feelings myself. On the one hand, it seems to me that the ads represent the entire initiative of independent adoption in a nutshell: *get the birth mother to pick you*! And I feel uneasy about that thrust. (At Golden Cradle, we also take out ads, but our emphasis is on reaching the birth mother and offering her a choice. That sits better with me.)

On the other hand, I know that advertising can be very effective, and I find myself answering critics of the ads in the same manner in which I respond to people who criticize Golden Cradle for advertising. To the woman who is troubled with an untimely pregnancy and who does not know where to turn, the ads can be a beacon of light along a dark and lonely road. Your advertisement can be beautiful. Having said that, I hasten to add that writing and placing your own ads, and taking the phone calls if and when they come, is not a cinch. If you're going to take this route, I'd like to offer some advice.

First, let's talk about the ad itself. Before you create your own ad, try to read several. You will find adoption ads in the classified section of *USA Today* and in local newspapers in communities across the country. Notice that many begin with two or three words, in large type, that attempt to capture the reader's attention: LET'S HELP EACH OTHER . . . LOVING HOME . . . CONSIDERING ADOPTION?

Keep in mind your intended audience: the birth mother and, in some cases, members of her family. As you choose the points you will make and the words you use, ask yourself: "If I were reading this, would I pick up the phone and call these people?"

Reread the samples that were provided earlier. Both are actual ads that appeared in the classified columns. Do you find yourself responding to one more than the other? If so, ask yourself why. Does the idea of raising a child in a rural setting seem appealing? Obviously, that's the impression of warmth that the writers were hoping to convey, along with the use of their first names—included so that the birth mother, reading the ad, would feel an immediate connection to them.

But what if you live in a city apartment? In that case, you may want to make mention of the fact that your home is convenient to parks, museums, many cultural activities. What you're trying to communicate, in capsule form, is your desire and ability to care for a child. The challenge, as I see it, is to find a way to express your need and your uniqueness as convincingly, and briefly, and *honestly* as possible. It's a little like those contests where you're asked to complete a sentence in twenty-five words or less. It doesn't seem too hard a task—until you actually sit down and try to come up with those twenty-five well-chosen words.

Should you include names in the ad and, if yes, what names should you use? I think you owe it to the birth parents to be honest without being foolish, and I advocate the use of first names (leaving you and the birth parents the option of how much you wish to reveal about yourselves later, if and when the initial contact should move forward toward adoption).

If you choose to use a fictitious name in the ad, I think the caller should be told that it *is* fictitious. I believe that every lie will eventually be found out. Think about what might happen if you deceive the birth mother now, and later she meets the child and learns that you hadn't been honest. That discovery is almost certain to color any relationship that might then develop between you. The way I see it, there's a difference between lying about adoption and engaging in a closed form of adoption that's been mutually agreed upon.

Placing the Ads

Once you complete your ad, the next decision you face is where to send it. Trying to come up with a list of newspapers that will accept your ad for publication *and* reach the desired audience is a daunting task. A number of adoption entrepreneurs sell lists, some of them already printed on mailing labels, and others will offer to place the ads for you—for an additional fee. That's not a shortcut I'm happy with. If you decide on pursuing an independent adoption, I think you need to be integrally involved in the process. Taking out ads can become very expensive, and it's important to know both *where* your money goes and *what* the response is: whether you're getting sufficient return on your investment.

If you decide to work with a lawyer who specializes in adoption, he or she should also be able to provide you with an up-to-date list of newspapers that accept adoption ads. Your task, then, is to go home, decide which papers you wish to advertise in (there's some feeling that the southern, southwestern, and western regions of the country yield better results than northern and eastern areas), and begin phoning one paper after another, long-distance.

Once you reach the newspaper's classified ad department and learn that they do accept adoption ads, the next thing you will want to know is what they charge—by word, by line, and how many words to a line. Running an ad is not a one-shot deal. To improve your chances of reaching your intended audience, you will probably want your advertisement to appear in the paper for at least two successive weeks. And because you don't want to put all your eggs in one basket, it's generally recommended that you use several outlets at a time. One lawyer I know of advises clients to advertise in a minimum of twelve newspapers. The costs add up quickly. It's not unusual for adoption hopefuls to spend two, three, as much as five thousand dollars or more on an advertising campaign. Keep in mind the fact that this expense is over and above the cost of any legal fees.

In addition to inquiring into the cost of running ads, you will want to know how many similar notices appeared in the paper during the previous week. If the answer is none, you might wonder whether this is a good outlet; if it's more than five or six, there might be too much competition.

Before accepting your advertisement, some newspapers require you to submit a notarized letter attesting to the fact that the individual or couple placing the ad is legitimately seeking to adopt a baby and is not in the business of baby brokering. It's a good idea to have such a letter ready.

Once you've placed an ad, ask to be sent tear sheets from the issues in which your notice appears in order to make sure that

Dealing with the Responses

Many specialists who counsel adoption hopefuls on where and how to place their ads also advise them to rent a post office box at which they can receive responses. Most suggest installing a private, unlisted second telephone number in their homes *before* placing the ads. It is that number which will appear in print. I think that's a good idea. For one thing, having a second number insures that the line will be available if and when the awaited call comes. It also allows the adopting parents to protect their own identity until, and if, the time arrives when both they and the birth mother decide to open up the relationship.

A single adoptive mother named Jean describes the telephone relationship that she developed, over time, with the birth mother of the child who ultimately became her adopted son. "It's a very weird relationship," she says. "There's so much you have to reveal about yourself. There's so much you want to learn about the birth mother, about the birth father if possible, and about the circumstances that caused the pregnancy. There's a lot of sharing that goes on and a lot of holding back. It's like no other relationship. It's both intimate and distant at the same time."

What you do after placing the ads is up to you. I've known some people to sit at home and wait for responses. I don't think that's a good idea. For one thing, waiting only adds to your anxiety. You might not have a long time to wait. (I know of one woman who heard about a baby within four days of placing her ad.) Then again, you might. (Another couple I know has been at the advertising game for over a year now, and they still haven't been successful.)

Be prepared for some intrusion. You might receive some obscene phone calls. You might get three crank calls at three o'clock in the morning. But the fourth call might be legitimate.

So what *do* you do? Make sure you have an answering machine that begins with the message, "Operator, this machine accepts collect calls," since you cannot be at the phone twenty-four hours a day *every* day, and you don't want to take the chance that someone will work up the courage to phone you only to be turned off by a ringing phone that is not answered. You also may want to add some variation of the following to your message: "Hello. You've reached Judy and Bill. [Or: "You've reached 123-4567," if you've decided against the use of names.] We're happy you called and we very much want to talk to you. Please leave a number where we can reach you, and we'll get back to you as soon as possible. If you do not wish to leave a number, please call back. Thank you."

When you do get to speak to the birth mother, what do you say? Here's what you *don't* say. You don't go into a game of twenty questions that's designed to put the birth mother on the spot: How old are you? When is the baby due? Is the birth father involved? Why are you planning adoption for this baby?

You *do* want the answers to these questions, but you also want to put the caller (and yourself) at ease. So try opening the conversation as you would if you were introducing yourself to someone who might become a friend. Tell the caller something about yourself and (if you're not a single applicant) about your spouse. Tell her something about your interests, your life-style, and the kind of life you envision for the child. Share your feelings about wanting to adopt a baby.

Ask the birth mother about how she's feeling. Ask: Are you getting medical care? Do you have a place to stay? (One of the first birth mothers whom I met had been thrown out of the house and was sleeping in a Dunkin' Donuts shop. I got her to a gynecologist, I arranged a place for her to stay, and *then* we talked.) Show concern for the birth mother as a person, not just as a childbearer. Ask a bit about the birth father. And listen carefully to what she has to say. Ask for her phone number so you can call her back. It's a good idea to keep a pad near the telephone at all times and take notes during the conversation. That way, you won't forget details.

Somewhere along the line, the birth parents will tell you what they want. Jean recalls receiving the following request from a married couple who responded to one of her ads. "We'll give you the baby," they said, "on condition that you agree to support us for a year."

"I didn't say 'Absolutely not,'" Jean says. "I didn't ask, 'How much will that cost?' I didn't negotiate. I just said, 'Call my lawyer,' and gave them her telephone number."

If you are working with an attorney, and if the party on the line seems interested in pursuing placement of a child with you, the best way to bring the telephone conversation to a close is to say, "I am interested. Please call my lawyer."

The next sticky point is wondering whether the person you've been speaking to will go ahead and make the call. Some birth mothers are not very sophisticated; others are savvy consumers. They're shopping. You may never hear from them again.

The upside of advertising is that you often can get babies much more quickly than by working with an agency. By and large, the ads do get responses. It is not unusual to hear about couples who take out ads in papers and get a baby within a few months.

The flip side of that are couples who spend upward of a year or longer and ten thousand dollars in ads, and get nowhere. What they do receive are obscene phone calls, and scare calls, and even calls from people who are working scams like the following: A young woman responded to an ad for a baby and arranged a meeting with the husband and wife. They flew her to their hometown for an interview. She was attractive, articulate, and obviously pregnant. They put her up at a motel for a week and gave her spending money (quite a lot of spending money) while they got in touch with a lawyer.

One morning, their calls to the young woman went unanswered. When they arrived at the motel, she was gone. They later learned that this same young woman was involved in two or three other "adoptions" and was trying to extort money from all the people involved for a baby she had no intention of giving up. She later had that baby in jail.

WORKING WITH A LAWYER

Many people feel much more comfortable in managing an independent adoption if they've enlisted the services of a competent attorney to whom they can look for counsel and appropriate intervention. "Attempting a private adoption becomes an all-consuming project," says one adoptive father. "In the beginning, my wife and I were just grateful to have someone to turn to for guidance. Once we located our birth mother, however, we felt it was very important to have someone who would evaluate and respond to her requests, who would handle the medical bills and housing expenses, and who would make sure that everything was on the up-and-up. There's a lot about the adoption process that can create anxiety—not the least of it is whether the birth mother will go ahead with her plan for placement. The way we looked at it, that part of the process was in God's hands, not ours. The rest of the details we left to our lawyer."

Just as I've cautioned you to work with an agency that's right for you, it is surely as important (if you choose to use an attorney as your intermediary) to find the lawyer who is right for you. Here's how to go about doing that:

- Talk to parents who have successfully adopted through a lawyer. (You won't have to look for the adoptive parent; once you acknowledge that you're thinking about adopting, they'll come out of the woodwork);
- If they don't come out of the woodwork, however, you can seek them out—and find them—at meetings of adoptive parent organizations or by contacting your local chapter of Resolve;
- Write or call your local bar association and request a list of lawyers specializing in adoption (note: that's only a start; you still want to look for a client's recommendation);
- Speak to your gynecologist or fertility specialist. Chances are good that he or she will know about lawyers who handle adoptions.

What to Ask the Lawyer

Although the process differs from attorney to attorney, most will arrange an appointment with you for an introductory

Pursuing an Independent Adoption

meeting. Be prepared to pay a nonrefundable consultation fee for this meeting, and use the time well. To help you decide whether working with a lawyer is right for you, and whether this is *the* right lawyer, I've listed several questions you will want to ask:

— How long has the lawyer been in practice? How many nonrelative adoptions has he or she handled in the past five years? (Or what percentage of the total practice is made up of adoption work?)

You are seeking to find out if adoption is a specialty of the lawyer's or simply a sometime thing.

— How many (or what percentage) of adoption cases handled by the lawyer failed to result in a successful placement? What went awry in these cases?

You want to see if the lawyer promises you a rose garden or if he or she is being realistic. You also want to assess your own chances of achieving a successful independent adoption.

— Is the lawyer reachable both day and night? How—and by whom—will calls from the birth mother be handled?

You want to be certain that it will be possible to reach your legal representative in an emergency, such as in case you get a call from a birth mother in the early hours of the morning, saying that she needs help. Once you decide to work with a particular birth mother and give her your lawyer's name and number as a go-between, you want to feel secure that any and all requests from the birth mother will be handled promptly, and with tact and understanding.

— If the baby is born in another state, will your lawyer be able to handle it? What is the lawyer's experience in managing interstate adoptions?

It's important that your lawyer understand how to

deal with the Interstate Compact on the Placement of Children, a uniform law that establishes specific procedures that must be followed when children are being transferred from one state to another. It's also helpful for your lawyers to have established contacts with attorneys and doctors in other states.

— Does the lawyer have strong feelings about openness or confidentiality in adoption? What are these feelings and how do they govern his or her practice?

A lawyer's brochure that recently came across my desk makes much ado about the importance to the adoptive parents of protecting their privacy, raising a question in *my* mind: Just how well would this lawyer work with a birth mother or with adoptive applicants who wanted to establish either one-time or ongoing contact with one another? On the other hand, what if privacy is important to you and the lawyer pressures you into accepting conditions of openness? My response in both situations is to find another lawyer, one whose philosophy more closely matches your own thoughts and desires.

— What efforts will the lawyer undertake to identify the birth father and inform him about the baby? How will those efforts be documented?

— Is the birth mother counseled as to her options? What about the birth father?

Some lawyers have social workers on their staffs whose job it is to work with birth mothers. Other attorneys refer birth parents to agencies that offer counseling. You *will* want to know that the birth parents are not being pressured to relinquish their parental rights; that theirs is a considered decision.

— How complete is the medical and social history that is gathered on the birth parents and their families? Are there provisions for follow-up?

— In general, what kinds of records are kept—and for how long? What will happen to those records if the lawyer goes out of business?

To some adoption applicants, these questions are important because they want to be sure that their privacy will be preserved. Others are interested in just the opposite. They want to assure that adoption records will be available to the adopted child if and when such information is desired.

— What happens if the infant is born with a serious condition (such as cystic fibrosis or Down's syndrome)? What does the lawyer have in place to ensure that the birth mother and baby receive appropriate services?

There are two issues to be considered here. First, you want to find out whether you'll be responsible for legal and medical expenses even if you decide against following through with the adoption. It's important to raise this matter early on in your negotiations. Second, you want to know that mother and child will not be abandoned. I think it's important, in selecting a lawyer, to make sure that you deal with someone who has a plan to meet these contingencies.

— What will the adoption cost? What are the lawyer's fees? Also remember to ask: what portion of the fee is nonrefundable if we fail to go through with the adoption—if a pregnancy occurs or we locate a baby through another means?

The lawyer can and should be able to tell you what his fee will be for legal services rendered and what those services will include. You should expect to be given that information *in writing*. Because so many of the expenses in an independent adoption (over and above the legal fee) must be borne by the adoptive parents themselves, don't fail to ask: What other adoption-related expenses might we encounter?

No lawyer will be able to provide you with an exact figure of what the adoption will cost. There are just too many variables, beginning with the cost of advertising for a birth mother and including: medical care for the birth mother and her baby (which can run quite high if the infant is delivered by cesarean section and even higher if the birth is premature); expenses for the birth mother, including food, clothing, telephone, or housing; travel arrangements if the birth mother chooses to have the baby away from her home state; fees paid to a second lawyer or agency when the adoption takes place in another jurisdiction or if the birth mother has her own lawyer. Remember, what's "allowed" depends on the laws of your particular state.

You will probably be asked to establish a special account with the lawyer's office out of which all expenses will be paid. The lawyer should furnish you with periodic, detailed information about how the money is spent.

After you leave the lawyer's office, think about the answers you received to your questions. Did they satisfy you? Did the lawyer seem to know her stuff, and were her answers straightforward? Did you feel pressured into signing on as a client? Did the lawyer make you aware of the emotional and financial risks of private adoption—did she tell you about what happens if the birth mother changes her mind and does not go through with the adoption? (What happens basically is that you're out the money you spent.)

Finally, ask yourself whether or not you *liked* the lawyer. Just as in choosing an agency, you must feel comfortable with the attorney you select to guide you through an independent adoption. A law firm or individual practitioner may have all the right credentials, but you might feel that the lawyer is insensitive . . . or sleazy. Trust your instincts. Don't agree to retain someone who will not make you feel pleased about the way in which you and your child are united. The kind of relationship you form with your lawyer can make a tremendous difference in how the adoption works out.

QUESTIONS THAT ARE LIKELY TO HAUNT YOU

Will I Be Chosen?

As you proceed with the process of adopting independently, this is the first of two questions that are most likely to haunt you. Here's how one adoptive mother describes the feeling of waiting to be "chosen": "It was a lot like when I was single and dating. I'd meet a boy, go out with him on Saturday night and think something good had taken place between us, then spend the next several days tied up in knots wondering if I was going to hear from him again. If he didn't phone, it hurt. Well, that's how it feels when you talk to a birth mother who sounds good to you. You get all excited. When she doesn't follow through, when she chooses a different couple for her child, it can really rip you apart."

While there's little that can be done about the birth mother's decision, I do believe that there is unnecessary cruelty in some of the selection methods being employed by certain adoption facilitators who are currently active in the independent adoption scene. In one situation, for example, the facilitators organize group sessions that bring together expectant birth mothers with individuals who are hoping to adopt. The stated purpose is for everyone to explore adoption, but in fact this is a kind of matchmaking service in which the birth parents are doing the choosing. When the birth parents announce their decision, selecting couple A over couple B, both couples are in the room. The one that has not been chosen is devastated. In deference to them, the "winning couple" must do its best to control their elation.

To minimize the pain of waiting to be chosen, I encourage you to refuse to become involved in any such programs. Once again, the guiding rule is: don't do anything that doesn't feel right.

What if the Birth Mother Changes Her Mind?

This is the other question that is likely to cause you sleepless nights. And not without reason. A woman whom I'll call Sarabeth looks back at an adoption agreement that failed: "Once we decided to adopt, my husband Gil and I placed ads in several papers, eventually hearing from a young woman in Texas. She told us she was in her eighth month, and that she'd made up her mind to place her baby for adoption. We asked a number of questions, liked her answers, and told her that we wanted to speak to her gynecologist before making any commitments. She agreed. We then had our lawyer get in touch with her doctor, who verified that the birth mother was pregnant and that she ought to have a normal delivery. We decided to go ahead.

"The birth mother told us she wanted all of the arrangements to be handled by our lawyer, which was acceptable to us," Sarabeth goes on. "We paid our lawyer's bill and covered her medical expenses, doctor *and* hospital. We also hired a private agency that would handle the adoption in Texas, and we quickly had a home study done by a social worker who'd been recommended by our lawyer. [Note: whether you adopt through an agency or independently, you will need to have a home study done.]

"The next time we heard from the birth mother, it was to tell us that she was in labor. Then we heard . . . nothing. Gil and I were on tenterhooks. We phoned the hospital for three days, but were unable to speak to the birth mother. Finally, we reached the gynecologist. He told us that the birth mother had walked out of the hospital with her baby. To say that we were devastated is to put the whole thing mildly. We also were out more than six thousand dollars."

Sarabeth adds, "I think people should be made aware that independent adoption has its pitfalls. I don't think people realize how difficult the process can be." The increased risk of disappointment and financial loss is certainly a possible downside of independent adoption. I'm not saying that pregnant women don't ever change their minds after stating an intention to relinquish their babies in agency-arranged adoptions, but in those cases the adopting couples seldom face the disappointment since they don't learn about the child who is intended for them until the infant is ready to be placed. And they do not invest (either emotionally or financially) in a baby that is not delivered.

I should tell you, however, that Sarabeth and Gil went on to adopt a son—also through an independent adoption, and using the services of the same lawyer. In this case, they spoke to the birth mother every week. Sarabeth even flew out to Texas (yes, it was Texas again) to assist in the delivery. She estimates that, all in all, she and her husband spent over thirty thousand dollars. Looking at their active little boy, they consider the money well spent.

12

Adopting a Child From Another Land

The overwhelming advantage of international adoption is the same as for every other method of adopting: once everything works out, it's wonderful to become a parent. The outstanding disadvantage, according to some, is the frustration encountered in having to work through *two* bureaucracies, to satisfy two or more sets of rules and regulations, and to make one's way through an alien land and culture to a child whom you hope will become your own.

Since I haven't been involved in intercountry adoption personally or professionally, I won't pretend to be able to give you a nuts-and-bolts primer on How to Do It. It's a complicated process, and there are others who are better qualified to guide you through its course. But some issues seem very clear to me, and I'd like to take this opportunity to lay them out for you.

A MATTER OF ATTITUDE

The way I see it, the critical question in deciding whether or not to pursue an intercountry adoption has to do with *attitude*. How important is it that your child look like you? One woman (I'll call her Betty) successfully adopted two children, the first, a son, through Golden Cradle and the second, a daughter, through a personal contact in Chile. "My husband and I are truly color-blind," explains Betty of the couple's decision to pursue a foreign adoption. "It has never mattered to us that our son is light and our daughter is dark or, for that matter, that neither of the children looks like either of us."

She adds, "If you're adopting from a foreign country, you *have* to be prepared for the fact that your child may look different from you and your family and that there are people—including some who are perfectly well-meaning—who are going to react to that difference."

She provides an example. "When my husband and I telephoned family and friends with news of our son's arrival, the first thing they said to us was 'Congratulations.' Three years later, we received news that our daughter had been born in Chile, and again contacted everyone to share our good news. *This* time the initial response we heard was, 'What does she look like?'"

Once the child joins your family, that question quickly becomes "*Who* does she look like?" Chances are, you're going to hear *this* one again and again.

Your kids don't have to be born abroad for you to encounter insensitive comments from strangers. Here's a personal example. My son Josh is blond, my daughter Abby is dark. I'm used to having people comment on how attractive they are. But how about this remark from a woman behind the counter of a local bakery, who pronounced, "Your kids are gorgeous. They don't even look like you."

"That's why they're gorgeous," I answered without skipping a beat, and went on to order half a dozen bagels.

Adoptive parents of foreign-born children tell me that the stares they get are not always so approving, nor are the comments tactful. Says fair-skinned, red-headed Norene, who adopted her coffee-hued daughter from India, "There's generally some lady in the check-out line at the supermarket who looks down at my daughter, looks up at me, and then looks around to see who the father might be.

"Other people are even less subtle," Norene continues. "They either ask me outright, 'Who is the father?' or they ask 'Is she your own?' by which they mean is my daughter adopted. They ask this *in front of* the child. You've got to learn how to field insensitive comments. If you're going to get defensive or uptight, foreign adoption may not be for you."

When people tell me they're considering intercountry adoption and ask my advice, I tell them "Fine." I then ask if they've given thought not just to the bull's eye (a baby) but to the circles around the bull's eye. One of those circles involves members of the extended family. Will *they* welcome a child whose features or complexion reflect his or her national origin?

Just as you've probably gone for years carrying around a picture in your mind's eye of the son or daughter you hoped to have someday, remember that your parents have been envisioning what their eventual grandchild would be like. Adoption requires both of you to do a little refocusing of that image. I'm not saying that grandparents are likely to have a hard time accepting the notion of a foreign-born grandchild. I *am* saying that the adoption stands a better chance of success if you have their support.

Beyond Babyhood

Another circle surrounding the bull's eye extends out to those years, beyond babyhood, when the son or daughter you adopt becomes a school child. Will you be willing to learn more about the culture of the child's native land? Have you given any thought to how you can help the child feel pride in his heritage when he has come so far from the land of his birth?

If you're considering foreign adoption, you might also want to make a mental leap into the child's teenage years. Do you live in a community that will be welcoming of young people who look different? If you're able to look ahead to years of parties and dating, do you think you'll be supportive if your youngster finds himself or herself excluded from certain social gatherings? (I'm not saying that it will happen, only that it *could* happen.)

The point of all of this self-questioning is to have you move beyond the romance of a *baby* into the reality of a human being who may encounter some distinct challenges while growing up in American society. If you feel that you're ready to join with the child in meeting those challenges, then foreign adoption should be pursued.

WHERE ARE THE CHILDREN?

One of the things you'll want to do, early on, is find out which nations are possible sources of adoptable children, and learn about the children and their needs. According to the **National Adoption Information Clearinghouse**, Korea, Central and South America, India, and the Philippines are the sources of most foreign-born children adopted by Americans. Each country has very different rules and a very different pool of children. A good way to begin your research, therefore, is to get in touch with The National Adoption Information Clearinghouse and ask about the current state of intercountry adoption.

The **International Concerns Committee for Children** (911 Cypress Drive, Boulder, Colorado 80303; 303-494-8333) publishes a *Report on Foreign Adoption*, which contains information on countries that are open to adoption by foreigners, and lists agencies and a few independent facilitators that are known to be reliable. Keep in mind that intercountry adoption programs change frequently. A twenty-dollar donation to ICCC brings you the report and ten updates in any given calendar year. (The committee also maintains a listing service of over five hundred foreign children with special needs who are waiting for families to adopt them.)

You may also wish to contact **Adoptive Families of America** at 3333 Highway 100 North, Minneapolis, Minnesota 55422 (612-535-4829). There is no charge for a general information packet, which includes a list of over two hundred agencies nationwide. A glance down the list will give you a good idea of agencies that handle foreign adoptions, which countries they can deal with, and the kinds of youngster available.

Your next step is to check with your state department of social services and its interstate compact officer to find out if any special procedures need to be followed in bringing home a child who's been adopted in a foreign country. It's a good idea to look into these matters early. That way, you're less likely to run into the problems down the line.

Then, get in touch with the consulate of the country in which you are interested. Ask whether intercountry adoption is permitted, and what the criteria are for adopting. (If the country requires applicants to be married and you're single, you'll know to look elsewhere. If they have set a minimum length of marriage at five years and you exchanged vows only two years earlier, move on.)

After you've narrowed your list to one or two countries, get in touch with the **Bureau of Consular Affairs** of the Department of State in Washington, DC (202-647-3666). Ask to be connected to the offices that deal with the countries in which you are interested and then request an update on the adoption situation in these countries. You ought to be able to find out about any illegal activity that has come to the Bureau's attention.

A LOOK AT THE PROCESS

Expect to find the road to intercountry adoption marked by detours and paved with paperwork. Sometimes a country that seems to be very open to placing its children abroad shuts down. This happened in Nicaragua, for example, when the Sandinistas overthrew the Somoza government. It happened in Paraguay, which decided that it was losing too many of the nation's future citizens to out-of-country adoption and abruptly put a stop to the practice. For men and women who were in the process of adopting from Nicaragua or Paraguay when these shutdowns occurred, this was another disappointment, another heartbreak on the road to parenthood.

You have to keep on top of the changing global situation and prepare to be rerouted if need be. Sometimes you'll find that a formerly locked and barricaded door has been thrown ajar, as recently occurred when the government of Nicolae Ceausescu was overthrown in Romania. Since the plight of hundreds of thousands of children in that nation became known, adoption programs have been inaugurated and many families and individuals have rushed to welcome available children into their lives. But even as I write this, the situation is in flux, with opportunists having come forward to take advantage of adoptive hopefuls who are flocking to this country. That's what I mean when I speak of detours and changes of direction. That's what I mean by booby traps.

Now, here's what I mean by paperwork. If you think that gathering documents for an in-country adoption is hard work, be prepared to go the distance for an international adoption. You'd better be very good at filling out forms, keeping records, and following up. (As a general rule, it's a good idea to proceed according to Murphy's law: expect that if anything can possibly go wrong, it will—and act accordingly.)

Be prepared. Even if you're only *thinking* about foreign adoption and have not yet contacted an agency, you will want to *start a file* and begin to assemble the following documents:

— birth certificates of the individuals who will be adopting;
— a copy of a divorce decree or death certificate of a deceased spouse (where applicable) to show proof of the end of the marriage;
— an employer's letter attesting to the fact that you're gainfully occupied; if self-employed, proof that you are in business, plus, in either case, copies of your W-2 forms, showing your income and net worth;
— a medical letter attesting to the state of your health (some countries also want proof of infertility);
— a copy of your fingerprints. One mother who has successfully negotiated the rigors of an international adoption now advises others, "When you go to the police station for fingerprinting, make sure that you have *two* copies made. That way, if the FBI calls to say that the thumb print on your left hand is not clear, you'll have another set of prints ready to submit, and won't have to go back to square one." This woman adds, "If possible, have your prints taken at the police station. Trying to get anything done at the INS—Immigration and Naturalization Service—is a hassle."
— a valid passport. You may have to travel to the country of adoption and stay there for weeks, possi-

bly months. It's no fun to get everything ready and *then* find that your passport has expired.

The reason for gathering some of the necessary documents early is so you'll be free to handle other of the requirements when the actual adoption process gets under way. I don't, for example, advise asking people to write recommendations for you until you know the specific nature of what's wanted by the foreign government, but I do suggest that you start *thinking* about people you might approach for a recommendation when the right time comes. It also can't hurt for you to have photographs taken of yourself, your home, and the room where the baby will reside . . . in case they will be needed.

In international adoption as in domestic adoption, you'll need to have a home study done and approved by a recognized agency. (Some agencies that facilitate foreign adoptions will only agree to work with you *after* you've submitted an application and a completed home study; others will take you on and *then* help you orchestrate the adoption.)

Not only will you have to gather the necessary documents, you'll also be expected to present them complete with all of the whistles and bells—that means certified, notarized, and delivered in triplicate. In foreign adoption, remember, you have to meet the adoption requirements of your home state, of the federal government, and of the country in which the child resides.

Be sure to keep track of all documents and correspondence. Make and keep copies of all the papers you mail out. Keep in mind that if anything *can* go wrong, it usually will. When disaster strikes, you'll still be able to consider yourself ahead of the game if you also don't have to retrace your steps through the paper trail.

And find a reliable translator. She'll come in handy.

AGENCY OR PRIVATE ADOPTION?

Some people are able to negotiate the intricacies of an international adoption on their own with relative ease. As a rule, these are people who have trustworthy personal contacts in the foreign country, who are able to speak the language, who are prepared to travel to that country for periods of time if need be, and who are willing to pretty much put the rest of their lives on hold while they assemble a lot of papers and walk them through domestic and foreign bureaucracies.

If you are working on your own with a lawyer or other independent facilitator in a foreign country, I urge you to proceed with caution. Ask to meet and speak with others who've adopted through your source. Try to stay on top of the process. Be sure you find out what the lawyer, the agency, the orphanage charges before going ahead. Find out what services these fees will cover. *Ask questions every step of the way.* If possible, get the answers in writing.

If you need to find a lawyer abroad, check with the American embassy in the country where you hope to adopt. United States lawyers handling foreign adoptions often have legal contacts abroad as well.

Generally speaking, I think it is better—and safer—to work with an agency that is familiar with handling intercountry placements, one that you've checked out and that you feel comfortable using. You want to be able to rely on experienced people to help you through the often long and complicated process. As best you can, you want to be able to minimize the risks.

A LOOK AT THE RISKS

Some of the risks in intercountry adoption have to do with the process—with the need to rely long-distance on foreign intermediaries to negotiate on your behalf for a child born in a strange and faraway land. "You feel so out-of-control," says a woman named Celia, who shares with us some of the ups and downs of her efforts to adopt a child from Latin America.

As part of the process of looking into adoption, Celia and her husband Neil attended a course at a local community college on how to adopt a child. "It was given by an attorney, a woman with whom we felt instantly comfortable and whom we later went to see about adoption," says Celia. "In our sessions with her, she introduced the idea of different types of children—older children, children of a race different from ours, children with certain illnesses or handicapping conditions—and asked us to consider the kind of child we'd feel comfortable with, and the situation we could handle.

"Guided by her, we began to look into adopting from Latin America," Celia continues. "We found that Costa Rica would not accept applications for children under the age of four. We hoped for a younger child. Honduras required adoption applicants to make a first trip to the country, then return—or to make only one trip and reside in the country for at least four months. We decided to pursue adopting from Paraguay, which only required a stay of one to two weeks. Our lawyer contacted an agency and we began assembling the necessary papers. Our adoption plans were well under way when Paraguay shut down.

"We then made contact with another agency, setting our sights and our hopes on Peru. Once we were assigned a child, we learned, we would have to spend six weeks in Peru before we could leave for home with the baby. We arranged our lives accordingly, and waited. Finally, there came the call we'd been waiting for. It was about a three-month-old child, Elena, who had been abandoned by her mother and was available for adoption. We were told that the little girl had light eyes and dark hair. We also were told that she weighed only eight pounds. Our hearts went out to this little girl at once. We immediately phoned our families, told them we had a daughter, and started to pack."

Celia continues, "We were literally out the door when the phone rang. We even debated for a moment whether to answer it. It was our contact from the agency again. Sorry, he said. Elena's mother had come back and reclaimed her child. We think that story is highly unlikely. We don't know what happened. We don't know if he'd been able to strike a better deal. The only thing we do know is that we were shattered.

"It's impossible to give you an adequate description of our feelings," says Celia. "There was anger . . . distrust of the agency . . . frustration . . . sadness . . . even mourning, because it felt as if a death had just occurred in our family. It's amazing how quickly your heart can claim a child as your own. And yet we were luckier than some other people we knew. We didn't make the trip to Peru and *then* return home with empty arms."

Celia and Neil have since adopted a child domestically.

Having recounted Celia's story, I should tell you that I also know of several intercountry adoptions that have gone smoothly from start to finish. The toughest part of these adoptions (and this is true of many intercountry arrangements) is that the adopters often have to wait several months between the time they learn that they've been assigned a particular baby and the time when they are legally able to pick that baby up and take her home. Some of the waiting time may have to be spent in the child's native country. Still, there's a silver lining to every cloud. One adopter I know sees this requirement as "one of the best things about foreign adoption." He explains, "Look at it this way, you not only get to go and bring your child home, you get to enjoy a southern vacation in the process."

Other risks of adopting foreign children have to do with shady dealings. The best way that I know of to protect yourself from getting caught up in dishonest schemes is to check on the references of anyone who is recommended to you—and on the source of those references. Parent groups, such as the **Latin America Parents Association** (LAPA) which has chapters in several states, are good places to inquire. Bad news travels fast, and chances are good that if somebody's been burned the grapevine has already caught wind of the incident.

The other way to protect yourself (by now I almost can hear you chanting this in unison with me) is to *trust your instincts*. If there's something about a person or situation that just doesn't feel right to you, extricate yourself as quickly as possible. Look for a different opportunity.

Health is another risk factor. A reputable agency or lawyer who's experienced in managing foreign adoptions ought to have good medical contacts in those countries in which they do business. It is possible that they'll be able to provide you with medical background on the birth parents as well as on the baby. One couple I know who adopted from the Philippines received a very clear history of the birth family, as well as Apgar scores taken of their daughter immediately after she was born. In most situations, however, adopting parents will have to be prepared for the information they receive on the child to be much more spotty. Also, much less accurate.

Once the child arrives home, it's not at all unusual for adoptive parents to discover that a boy or girl who's been described as "healthy" is, in fact, in need of medical attention. You may find that your foreign-born child weighs less than the baby next door or that he or she may take longer to reach some of the developmental milestones. (It's fairly safe to assume that the birth mother may have had little or no medical care during her pregnancy.) A change in diet may also cause problems for the child. (Lactose intolerance is common among Hispanic and Asian infants.)

Children who arrive here from foreign countries may suffer from conditions that are quite common in their native communities but are rarely found in the United States. Some are troubled by worms or other digestive disorders that are not easily diagnosed by American doctors who are not unused to seeing these conditions. Locating a pediatrician who's had some experience in treating these ailments can go far in easing the discomfort of your child, as well as allaying some of your own fears and concerns.

In time, the children begin to settle in. They grow comfortable in their new settings and with their new families. The parents who have adopted internationally tell me that they, too, find themselves growing and thriving—often in ways they hadn't anticipated.

"In meeting our son or daughter's need to know and feel pride in their origins, in learning with them about their culture," these parents say, "we have extended our own boundaries. In a very real sense, we now see ourselves as international families, individuals who have chosen to adopt one another's culture as our own."

Now *that's* what I call an upside of adopting.

13

How Do You Keep From Going Nuts While You Wait?

Up to now, this book has focused strongly on the importance of persistence in attaining your goal. I've make it very clear, I hope, that (no matter which of the roads you choose toward adoption) persistence will lead you to that road and perseverance will help you follow it to a successful conclusion. Now I'd like to talk to you about a contrasting situation, *waiting*, which may well turn out to be the most frustrating part of the entire adoption process.

I'd like to try to help you through it.

When You're Starting Out

You will experience periods of lows and highs throughout your journey to adoptive parenthood. Waiting isn't easy. First you'll find yourself waiting to find out whether an agency will accept your application and agree to work with you . . . or waiting to see if a birth mother will be drawn to *your* biography among others and choose the two of you as the future parents of her expected child. There's waiting to find out if the person who responded to your ad will follow through and phone you again or get in touch with your lawyer. Sometimes all of this waiting, to see whether anything *will* happen, whether your hopes and dreams are going to be able to get off the ground, can become unbearable.

At those times, you can feel very discouraged. You may wonder whether to give up. You may cry. You may become so frustrated that you'll feel like striking at someone or something. Try a punching bag. I'm not kidding. That's what I did when the waiting got so bad that I felt I could no longer endure it. And it helped.

If the bad moments hit you as a couple, try taking a drive to the beach and walking together along the shore. That's the sort of thing that can have a calming effect on you when just about everything else fails. If only one of you is low, take the drive by yourself and find the serenity that will help you get on top of your feelings. What you don't want to do is to take your frustration out on your partner. You need each other more than ever now.

You also need others. That's why I encourage every person who's in the process of adopting to develop a relationship with a "buddy" couple or single adoptive parent who can support you when you're feeling low and who can answer the "dumb" or "touchy" or "sensitive" questions that you're either embarrassed or afraid to ask your case worker or lawyer. At Golden Cradle, we try to match our adoption applicants with a resource couple who live in their area, a husband and wife who've already been through the process.

We ask our resource people to make themselves available to receive phone calls from the anxious couple, to share their own experiences (both positive and negative), to encourage couples to speak to the social worker when problems arise, and to respect the confidentiality of what is being told to them. We do not expect the buddy couple to serve in the place of professionals; we do hope they will serve the adopting couple as friends.

If you're working with an agency that doesn't have a program like this in place, ask if they can put you in touch with couples in your area who have adopted. You'll be glad you did.

If you're doing a private adoption, you can still develop a network through membership in an adoptive parents organization where you will get to know men and women who have lived your experience or who are currently going through it and who understand what you're feeling. They may be able to offer concrete advice about what your next step should be. Or they can just listen. At times, that may be the biggest help. (I think that joining such an organization can be helpful whether you're adopting privately or through an agency. As you go about the business of raising your adopted child, you'll find that your fellow members continue to be a source of friendship and support for the family. Both are important.)

Keep reading. Many good books have been written about adoption—books on how to adopt, about first-person experiences, and about special issues to consider in raising an adopted child. (See suggested reading list on page 203.) Reading about adoption is not only a way to gain information, it is also a good way to find some common ground when you need it, to connect with an author who understands.

Keep busy. Remain active in your job. If you have a hobby or favorite extracurricular activity, this is the time to pursue it. Volunteer. I've found that getting involved in worthwhile communal activities is good. Focusing on others' needs, and doing something to help meet them, is the best way that I know of to take the spotlight off yourself and your own concerns. I recommend it.

Once You've Been Accepted

In the beginning, it's all hopping and jumping. There's so much to do: meetings to attend; autobiographies to write; financial papers to assemble; recommendations to procure. You long for a restful period. And then you get your wish.

The hard part that you and your spouse may not be prepared for is the time when you're just coasting, when you've been approved for adoption by an agency . . . when you've filed all the necessary papers with the lawyer . . . when you hear that a child has been selected for you half-way across the world, and you're told that *all* you have to do is wait.

Are they kidding?

At Golden Cradle, we know how difficult this period can be. We know how you feel because you've told us. Here, in a letter written to the agency, is how one waiting parent describes this period:

> How hard it has become! What seemed like it was going to take no time at all has taken an eternity. Or so it seems. We all have had the misfortune to have suffered through failed pregnancies, medications, and surgeries. We have all shed too many tears for too many disappointments. Why then, after all of this, when the most promising situation we may ever have takes a little longer than expected, are we so distraught and frustrated? . . . We are not used to waiting without having something bad happen. We are not used to having a situation that will turn out all right. We have become conditioned to disappointment.
>
> We walk the day with a heavy load upon our shoulders. . . . Every time the phone rings, our hearts pound. Every time we play back our answering machine, our stomachs begin to churn. But the worst part of this wait is the question that everybody asks every time we speak to them: "So, what's new?" . . . One day I hope to be able to tell them that something is new!

Rest assured, that day *will* come. Until it does, however, here are some suggestions about what you can do to spend the waiting time constructively . . . and to keep from going nuts.

- Do something concrete to prepare for the baby's arrival. Knit a sweater, refinish a bassinet, paper the nursery.
- Child-proof your house. Are the rugs skid-proof? Check to see that smoke detectors have been installed in all the rooms and are in working order.
- Keep a journal. Use it as a way to chart your feelings, explore your ups and downs, fears, frustrations, and

anticipations. (Someday you may wish to share this with your child.)
- Take a course in parenting.
- If your agency or lawyer has not already required it, sign up for a course in infant cardiopulmonary resuscitation (CPR) now. Treat it as a matter of life or death.
- Take a course in anything that interests you, from macramé to money management.
- Begin reading a 400-page novel, or go back to the classics. Who knows how long it wil be before you have the opportunity again?
- Choose a name for the baby. This activity has kept some couples going for months.
- Decide who the godparents will be.
- Decide on the wording and style of your adoption announcement. This will enable you to place your order as soon as your son or daughter arrives, and get the good news out quickly.
- Make a list of pediatricians. Take the time to contact and interview them *now* so you'll know where to go when your child arrives. (Most adoptive parents like the reassurance of having a local doctor examine the infant soon after the baby's arrival and hearing those magical words, "The baby is fine.")

If you're involved in an intercountry adoption, you may find it useful to identify a pediatrician who can help make some sense out of the medical information you receive on a particular child. If the doctor cautions against the adoption, ask why. Often the adopting couple is able to handle challenges that the doctor might not personally be willing to accept.

As a rule, it's a good idea to find out how the doctor feels about adoption. One woman recalls being asked by a pediatrician she was interviewing, "Is it definite, then, that you and your husband are unable to have a child of your own?" The husband and wife went on to find another "doctor of their own" for the baby who soon after joined their family by adoption.

- Line up child care, if necessary. Develop a list of reliable baby sitters in the neighborhood.
- If you don't have a will, make one. If you do have a will, consider making some changes.
- Review your insurance policies. You may want to make some changes here, too.
- Savor the peaceful moments. Take advantage of the opportunity to enjoy a full night's sleep. Once the baby comes (and no matter how happy you'll be to at long last have an occupant in the nursery), I can promise you that there'll be times when you'll actually find yourself longing for the peace and quiet that you have right now.
- Take a vacation (a week at a country inn or a weekend orgy of show-going in the center of a big city). Have a wonderful time, but make certain to tell the agency or lawyer that you're going out of town and where you can be reached. Because (take my word for it) sometime when you least expect it . . . when you've made up your mind to tackle a project you've been putting off . . . when you've finally decided to stop sitting by the phone and to go away for a weekend . . . when you've almost reached a point where you're resigned to the wait, you *will* be contacted with the news that your long wait for a baby is over.

At Golden Cradle, that phone call always begins with . . . *"Hello. This is the Stork calling. I have a delivery to make."*

Afterword

Dear Agency:

First of all, I want to express my appreciation for the important services you perform. Adoption agencies have been greatly (and often unjustly) maligned in recent years by critics who failed to place the agencies' past policies within the context of the times in which they were practiced.

Not so very long ago, for example, communities could be pretty tough on unmarried mothers *and* on the children they bore. So it wasn't too surprising that, when a young woman found herself confronted with an unplanned pregnancy and looked for ways to avoid the stigma that society attached to the situation, either she or her family (and often both) turned to adoption agencies for help.

And the agencies came through: placed the mother in a maternity home where she'd be free from the stares and whispers of her community; found a home for the baby with a couple who longed to raise a child and were able to take on the rights and responsibilities of parenthood; and promised everybody involved that their secrets would be safe. In the context of history, we cannot fault agencies for their discretion.

There was a time, too, when the number of adoptable babies was more in sync with the population of people who were eager to adopt. This meeting of supply and demand came about largely *because* an unmarried woman was discouraged from raising the child who had been born to her. It was thought that placing the baby for adoption would be better both for her sake and for the sake of the child. As a result, agencies did not find themselves having to turn away so many adoptive applicants away. But those times and those circumstances have changed dramatically.

Unfortunately, I find that some agencies still cling to "the good old days" when they alone made the tough decisions and the clients thanked them for it. One veteran caseworker complained to me recently, "I remember a time when the birth mothers would be *grateful* for our seeing them. Today they tell us, 'I'll let you know *if* I decide to go ahead.'"

Instead of tiptoeing through the back door of adoption agencies, birth parents are striding through the front door; they are asking questions; they are shopping around. Dear Agency, you must be open to the challenge, constantly reevaluating your policies and practices to see that they not only reflect today's reality but that they respond to it.

Above all, don't mistake the style for the substance. Birth parents still need your help, but differently. More and more, they do not turn to agencies to decide for them, but rather to assist them in considering their decision, or in implementing it. They still have questions, still struggle with uncertainties, still waver about what course of action will be best for them and their child.

You have to be sensitive to those feelings from the time that people make their initial contact with your agency. You don't want anyone to be turned off . . . and to quickly turn away. For starters, then, it's important to pay attention to the way people are treated during the critical first phone call that they place to your agency.

If you want to know whether the welcome mat is really out, try phoning your agency from the outside sometimes. Listen to how the call is received. See how you're treated when you identify yourself as a birth mother . . . or as someone who is anxious to adopt. Believe me when I tell you that these spot checks can be *very* instructive.

Here's how I know. From time to time, I place calls to various adoption agencies. Sometimes the phone will ring fifteen times before it is picked up. (How many people are willing to wait through fifteen rings? When my call *is* answered, I say that my wife and I are interested in adopting, and wait for a response. I have to tell you that the answers I receive are no warmer and no more humane now than they were when that was truly my situation and I felt so vulnerable.

Dear Agency, you have to give people more information than the fact that "intake is closed." You have to tell them when intake will be reopened. You should also be able to refer callers to a support group. You have to give people some reason to hope.

If you think your agency has a quicker and warmer response when the person on the line is calling to speak about the possibility of *placing* her baby, think again. I recently phoned one agency and identified myself as a birth father. I said, "The woman who's going to have my baby and I are considering adoption." I was told, "The worker who handles adoption is out in the field. Call back later."

I phoned another agency. This time I posed as a father who was seeking help for his daughter. "My daughter and her three-month-old are here with me," I said. "Her boyfriend has deserted her. We'd like to talk to you about adoption."

The response I got was, "We'll take your name and get back to you."

In one such test, I never received a return phone call from the agency. In another, the call came two weeks later. "Sorry," I said. "My daughter's child has already been placed."

You get the point.

Dealing with Birth Parents

We must keep in mind that there are many pressures on the women—and men, too—who find themselves confronted by an unintended pregnancy. There have always been pressures on the women to place their children for adoption. Nowadays, there may be even more pressure on them to keep the babies than to plan adoptive placements. There may be pressure to abort. If adoption is a possibility, the birth parents want information about how it will be arranged. They need to be informed so they can make an intelligent choice.

I cannot speak too strongly about the importance of options counseling, of helping parents-to-be look at their situation and at the supports that are available to them so that they can reach a decision that will be best for them and the child. If they decide against placement, you will have the satisfaction of knowing that parent and child stand a better chance of making it because you have helped the parents think through, and plan for, their future.

If adoption is the option that's chosen, involve the birth parents in selecting the kind of family they would like their baby to grow up in. Organize support groups for birth parents within your agency. (It's a good idea, if possible, to have birth mothers represented on your staff and board of directors. At Golden Cradle, our practice continues to benefit from the special insights they contribute.)

Keep the agency door open. Make sure that the birth mother knows that she can come back for counseling or just to talk, and that she will be welcome to inquire about the baby's welfare. In recent years, more and more agencies have started offering post-adoption services to their clients. That's because we've been learning (although gradually) that adoption is a lifelong process for *all* of the parties involved: the birth parents and their families; the adoptive parents and their families; the adopted children who are likely to have questions and who may need some added support throughout their growing-up years and even beyond. It should be the agency's mission to remain part of that process if the parties desire it.

Dealing with Adoptive Applicants

The same sense of openness and cooperation must be extended to the adoptive couples or single applicants with whom you work. It's important to see the agency's role as not only encompassing evaluation but also education. Help your applicants become partners in the decision-making process.

I'm concerned that certain people who are eager to adopt a baby will agree to just about any condition the agency imposes, even though they may have reservations about some of those conditions. Today, when openness is the rule rather than the exception, people who apply to adopt should be educated to the varying degrees of openness, should be helped to consider their relationship to the birth parents and to the child, and should be encouraged (but not prodded) to come to an informed decision that feels right to them.

I also believe that all agencies must offer workshops on the special issues that may be encountered by adoptive parents or by their children as they go on to live their lives together.

Respecting Your Responsibility to the Children You Place

In a large sense, you discharge that responsibility best in providing the best possible services and counsel to both the birth and adoptive parents. In addition to providing postadoption services to those children who want them *at any time that they might want or need them*, the agency has an ongoing responsibility to maintain good records that can be made available to the children when and as warranted.

Advertise

Make it easy for people to find you. Reach out into the community to let people know about your services and the quality and qualifications of your staff. Let them know that when they need someone or someplace to turn to, your agency can and will help.

Go Public About Adoption

Don't limit your efforts to publicizing the work of the agency. Tune in to the media. When you see a program about adoption, respond to it. Write letters to the editor. Offer to have representatives of your agency appear on talk shows.

When I first entered the world of agency adoption, it was a closed, private, don't-let-anybody-know-about-what-we're-doing world. Well, that's changed for the better, thank heavens, but we can't get complacent. Vestiges of that world remain. Even if intake is full, even if you quake at the thought of encouraging a barrage of phone calls that will have to be answered by your already overworked staff, you have to continue to bring the news of adoption to the public. The more often this positive form of building a family is stressed—the more that people hear about adoption and learn to feel comfortable with the subject—the better the climate will be for all concerned: birth parents, adoptive parents, and especially the children.

After all, the desire to attain that goal is what led most of us to work in this field in the first place, isn't it?

Affectionately,

Arty Elgart

Appendix I

National Adoption Resources

Adoptive Families of America
3333 Highway 100 North
Minneapolis, MN 55422
(612) 535-4829

Adoptive-parent support organization with particular knowledge of intercountry adoption. A free general-information packet on agencies that do adoption is available.

The CAP Book
700 Exchange Street
Rochester, NY 14608
(716) 232-5110

Publishes photographs and brief descriptions of children across the country who are waiting to be adopted.

Child Welfare League of America
Suite 301
440 First Street, NW
Washington, DC 20001
(202) 638-2952

A national organization for child welfare advocacy and education. Conducts research; publishes books and pamphlets on child welfare issues. Provides information on publications, list of member agencies.

Committee for Single Adoptive Parents
P.O. Box 15084
Chevy Chase, MD 20815

Provides helpful information for single people interested in adoption opportunities. Publishes *The Handbook for Single Adoptive Parents*.

International Concerns Committee for Children
911 Cypress Drive
Boulder, CO 80303
(303) 494-8333

Offers an information service on adoptable domestic and foreign children, an overseas orphanage sponsorship program, and an annual report on foreign adoption.

National Adoption Center
1218 Chestnut Street
Philadelphia, PA 19107
(215) 925-0200 or 1-800-TO-ADOPT

Provides information about special-needs adoption, registers children waiting for adoption as well as adults who have expressed interest in adopting children whose needs require special care. Helps facilitate interagency placements.

National Adoption Information Clearinghouse
Suite 1275
1400 Eye Street, NW
Washington, DC 20005
(202) 842-1919

The clearinghouse was established by Congress to provide the public with easily accessible information on all aspects of infant and intercountry adoption and the adoption of children with special needs. The clearinghouse does not place children for adoption or provide counseling. It does make referrals for such services. Also available from the clearinghouse is the *National Adoption Directory*, which contains lists of adoption agencies by state, parent support groups, adoption exchanges, and legal resources.

National Committee for Adoption
1930 17th Street, NW
Washington, DC 20009
(202) 328-1200

An organization of private adoption agencies that monitors legislation, counsels individuals and agencies on matters having to do with pregnancy, infertility, and adoption. Publishes the *Adoption Factbook*.

National Resource Center for Special-Needs Adoption
P.O. Box 337
Chelsea, MI 48118
(313) 475-8693

Provides publications, training, and technical assistance on the adoption of special-needs children to organizations and individuals.

North American Council on Adoptable Children
Suite N-498
1821 University Avenue
St. Paul, MN 55404
(612) 644-3036

Holds an annual conference and is a clearinghouse for adoptive-parent support groups nationwide. Emphasis is on the children who wait to be adopted.

Resolve, Inc.
5 Water Street
Arlington, MA 02174
(617) 643-2424

Membership organization providing services to infertile couples at both the national level and through state and regional chapters. Adoption information is offered.

Appendix II

Suggested Reading

You will find many books on adoption at your local library or book store. I have asked the members of Golden Cradle's staff to assist me in directing readers to those works which, in their opinion, are likely to be the most helpful. Their suggestions follow.

For General Information About Adoption

Adoption: Parenthood Without Pregnancy by Charlene Canape. A how-to-adopt book that manages to touch on the basic issues.

An Adoptor's Advocate by Patricia I. Johnston. The goal of this book is to help humanize the adoption process. This is not a how-to book. It is, however, a useful tool to understanding adoption.

Ideal Adoption: A Comprehensive Guide to Forming an Adoptive Family by Shirley C. Samuels. Offers a practical look at the entire adoption process, and gives the reader much to think about.

The Adoption Resource Book by Lois Gilman. True to its name, this book is a valuable resource for prospective and current adoptive parents. A wealth of material is presented in a well organized and clearly written manner.

The Psychology of Adoption, edited by David M. Brodzinsky and Marshall D. Schechter. Provides up-to-date information on research being done in adoption, primarily in the area of mental health. Although written for a professional audience, the book contains insights that the general reader may also find valuable.

For a Specialized Audience

Adopting the Older Child by Claudia Jewett. For anyone considering the challenge of adding an older child to the family, this book raises some critical issues and provides direction.

How to Adopt From Central and South America by Jean and Heino Erichsen. The title says it all.

The Handbook for Single Adoptive Parents, ed. by Hope Marindin. Although written as a general resource for the growing number of single adopters, the book contains sound advice that all prospective and current adoptive parents will find useful.

Understanding My Child's Korean Origins by Hyun Sook Han. A useful guide for anyone planning a Korean adoption.

Birth Family/Adoptive Family Relationships

Adoption: A Handful of Hope by Suzanne Arms. Stories of birth mothers and adoptive families and how open adoption has affected their lives.

Adoption Without Fear, ed. by James L. Gritter. First-person narratives help the reader understand what the term "open adoption" really means.

An Open Adoption by Lincoln Caplan. The process of adopting and the complex relationships that develop among the parties are explored in this true-life case history of an open adoption.

Dear Birthmother: Thank You for Our Baby by Kathleen Silber and

Phyllis Speedlin. One of the earliest works to deal with open adoption, the book contains actual letters exchanged between members of adoptive families, children, and birth parents. If you're considering an open adoption, this book provides food for thought.

The Adoption Triangle: Sealed or Open Records? How They Affect Adoptees, Birth Parents, and Adoptive Parents by Arthur Sorosky, Annette Baran, and Reuben Pannor. A landmark work in adoption when it appeared in 1978, the book has been revised to include current adoption policies. It remains relevant, and is highly recommended.

Living With Adoption

How to Raise an Adopted Child by Judith Schaffer and Christina Lindstrom. The authors, both psychotherapists, cover a wide range of situations that adoptive parents are likely to encounter at various stages of child rearing.

Lost and Found: The Adoption Experience by Betty Jean Lifton. A strong and cogent work that argues for the rights of adoptees to search for and know their birth origins.

Raising Adopted Children by Lois Ruskai Melina. Contains practical and authoritative advice on the special issues that come up in raising adopted children. A helpful and supportive book.

When Friends Ask About Adoption by Linda Bothun. Addressing sensitive issues, this book would make a good gift for friends and relatives of families formed by adoption.